THE LIBRARY OF HOLOCAUST TESTIMONIES

A Life Sentence of Memories

The Library of Holocaust Testimonies

Editors: Antony Polonsky, Martin Gilbert CBE, Aubrey Newman,
Raphael F. Scharf, Ben Helfgott

Under the auspices of the Yad Vashem Committee of the Board of
Deputies of British Jews and the Centre for Holocaust Studies,
University of Leicester

A Life Sentence of Memories

Konin, Auschwitz, London

ISSY HAHN

With a Foreword by Theo Richmond

VALLENTINE MITCHELL
LONDON • PORTLAND, OR

First Published in 2001 in Great Britain by
VALLENTINE MITCHELL
Crown House, 47 Chase Side
Southgate, London N14 5BP

and in the United States of America by
VALLENTINE MITCHELL
c/o ISBS, 5804 N. E. Hassalo Street
Portland, Oregon 97213-3644

Website: http://www.vmbooks.com

British Library Cataloguing in Publication Data
Hahn, Issy
   A life sentence of memories: Konin, Auschwitz, London. –
   (The library of Holocaust testimonies)
   1. Hahn, Issy 2. Jews – Poland – Konin 3. Refugees, Jewish –
   England – London 4. Holocaust, Jewish (1939–1945) – Personal
   narratives
   I . Title
   940.5'318'092

ISBN 0-8530-3415-X
ISSN 1363-3759

Library of Congress Cataloging-in-Publication Data
A catalog record for this book is available from the Library of
Congress

Typeset by FiSH Books, London.
Printed in Great Britain by MPG Books Ltd, Bodmin, Cornwall.

Contents

Dedicated to my friend,
my companion, my partner through hell, fire and water,
my dear brother Karol, who
passed away in 1993 after heart surgery.
He is truly missed.

List of Illustrations

Between pages 114 and 115

14. The author (right) with brother Karol in Warsaw, 1946.

15. The author with another survivor travelling to England on the Swedish Red Cross ship *Ragne*.

16. Rabbi Dr Solomon Schonfeld, with whom in 1946 the author travelled to England.

17. The author's Aunt Gittla, his mother's sister, London 1939.

18. The Kazimierz Forest, where the SS executed hundreds of men, women and children.

19. Mass grave of Jews murdered by the Nazis in 1942 at Wilkuf (near Konin), site of a Polish Christian cemetery.

20. The author at one of the five graves in Kazimierz Forest, site of mass execution of Jews from Konin (photograph by Theo Richmond).

21. Mushrooms growing in the Kazimierz Forest. Polish girls found gold rings and other jewellery on top of mushrooms that had pushed out of the ground.

22. Catholic icons inside the author's Aunt Golda's friend's house, when he visited her in 1987 on his return to Konin.

23. The author designed this symbol of his experience. The circle represents enclosure and loss of freedom, the stripes represent the camp uniform and the triangle with the letter 'P' represents either a Political or Polish prisoner.

Biographical Note

Issy Hahn was born in Konin, Poland, on 8 January 1927. He was a coal miner, cattle drover, construction worker, gravedigger and assembly line worker in a tank factory, all before the age of 18 – jobs not of his own choice, but that of the German Gestapo during the Second World War. In September 1942 he was deported to Auschwitz extermination camp. He remained there for four months and was selected to carry out forced labour in the coalmines of another concentration camp called Jaworzno. After 11 months there, he was sent on a three-week death march to Blechhammer concentration camp. Hundreds of men, women and children either died from the extreme cold or were shot by the German SS, but Issy survived. In March 1946 he came to England, where he met his wife, and worked in the meat industry for over 40 years.

The Library of Holocaust Testimonies

It is greatly to the credit of Frank Cass that this series of survivors' testimonies is being published in Britain. The need for such a series has long been apparent here, where many survivors made their homes.

Since the end of the war in 1945 the terrible events of the Nazi destruction of European Jewry have cast a pall over our time. Six million Jews were murdered within a short period; the few survivors have had to carry in their memories whatever remains of the knowledge of Jewish life in more than a dozen countries, in several thousand towns, in tens of thousands of villages, and in innumerable families. The precious gift of recollection has been the sole memorial for millions of people whose lives were suddenly and brutally cut off.

For many years, individual survivors have published their testimonies. But many more have been reluctant to do so, often because they could not believe that they would find a publisher for their efforts.

In my own work over the past two decades, I have been approached by many survivors who had set down their memories in writing, but who did not know how to have them published. I realized what a considerable emotional strain the writing down of such hellish memories had been. I also realized, as I read many dozens of such accounts, how important each account was, in its own way, in recounting aspects of the story that had not been told before, and adding to our understanding of the wide range of human suffering, struggle and aspiration.

With so many people and so many places involved, including many hundreds of camps, it was inevitable that the historians and students of the Holocaust should find it difficult at times to grasp the scale and range of the events.

The publication of memoirs is therefore an indispensable part of the extension of knowledge, and of public awareness of the crimes that had been committed against a whole people.

Martin Gilbert
Merton College, Oxford

Foreword

Many survivors of the Holocaust say they owe their lives to luck. For some, a Nazi nod in one direction granted life, a nod in the other sentenced their parents to death. Others happened to be gathering berries in the woods on the morning the SS rounded up the Jews of their village and massacred them in a nearby quarry. Luck certainly played a part in Issy Hahn's survival, but after talking to him at length and reading his book, I am convinced – as I think most readers will be – that much of the luck was self-created, the product of his resourcefulness, audacity, ability to think fast on his feet, and readiness to take risks that others drew back from. Issy illustrates better than anyone I know the truth of Louis Pasteur's dictum: 'luck favours the prepared mind.'

When the deportation train carried him away from his home town of Konin in November 1939, Issy was only a boy, but a grown-up boy, street-wise and physically tough. Blond hair and Polish looks added to his advantages in the survival game. Above all, what helped sustain him in the darkest hours of the ghettoes and concentration camps and during the death marches, was his refusal to accept defeat, his unwavering conviction that he would overcome and live to tell the tale: 'I don't know why but I was never frightened of anything because I never believed I could be killed.' For over five years this faith in his own destiny helped save not only his own life but that of his younger brother Karol, from whom he refused to be separated. It enabled him to embark on a series of daredevil exploits, not the least of which was his astonishing – though temporary – escape from Auschwitz.

That he came through so much unspeakable horror and suffering, so many brushes with death, is cause enough for wonder. But what arouses one's admiration too is his inner strength in dealing with the loss and grief that awaited him after liberation. Returning to Konin, he found his worst fears confirmed: the town he remembered, and its people, were gone. Uprooting himself from the land of his birth, arriving penniless in London, a strange city whose language he did not speak, he found work, married, had children and rebuilt his life. But he never forgot what he had endured, or the millions who had been murdered. This book is his testimony.

Theo Richmond, author of *Konin: A Quest*

'How did Hitler miss you? What did you come back here for? He missed you, didn't he?' The words came crashing through 40 years of memories and pounded my brain as I relieved myself on the weathered tombstone. The burial site was all but forgotten, grown high with weeds, in a secluded wooded spot outside Konin. I never could get this bastard out of my mind, but I never expected to stumble upon his grave either. 'Look where you are now, Wladek Morowski! You see who's under the ground and who's still alive!'

1 · The Germans Arrive in Konin

Konin lies on the banks of the River Warta between Poznań on the west and Łódź and Warsaw on the east. Its population in the summer of 1939 was around 13,000 – of whom 2,500–3,000 were Jewish. My family was quite large then and most of my extended family were born, and still lived, in Konin. My immediate family consisted of me, known to everyone as Srulek (11); my brothers Karol (ten) and Zalman (nine); my sister Malka (seven); and my mother Helena and my father Szymak.

The weather was good that summer and the people of Konin were going about their business as usual. It was June when I first noticed lots of people standing around open restaurant windows, the owners of which had positioned their radios there so people could hear news broadcasts from Radio Warsaw. I stood among the crowds of people listening to what was being said about the war. And there was plenty to hear. All Hitler's speeches were translated into Polish but now and again someone would switch the radio to a station from Berlin and I could hear Hitler himself screaming threats of war in German.

There was no reliable source of information. Not everyone had a radio and the *Polish Daily* was the only newspaper available. The paper carried rumours that Poland's foreign minister, Beck, who was in Berlin at the time, was revealing Poland's secrets and working with Hitler – not to stop a war, but to start one. The Polish people were simple, not knowing whom to trust, because they didn't know the truth. No one in Poland knew what was going on in Germany, but the Germans knew what was going on in Poland. They knew it would be no problem to take Poland.

As a boy of 11 I was only interested in playing with my friends. I didn't care about any war. We laughed about it. A war would bring a bit of excitement to our dreary town. We had no idea what was about to happen to our lives.

1

By mid-summer there were new faces in Konin. Smartly dressed people who drove Mercedes and BMWs milled about the town spreading rumours about war and bombs that would fall from the sky. My parents said they were German intelligence agents going from town to town trying to cause panic.

In August, a policeman on a bicycle knocked on our door and asked for my father; he came to deliver call-up papers for the Polish army. Most able-bodied men were being called to join the army, including my father's two brothers and my mother's three brothers. The men were expected in Warsaw immediately.

The very next day they were in my parents' house packing their rucksacks with food for the journey. My grandfather arrived with his horse and carriage to take them to the railway station. My uncles and father climbed into the carriage and I jumped in the front to sit beside my grandfather. He touched the horses lightly with his whip and we headed off to the station. He often let me ride with him while he worked, taxiing people back and forth from the railway station or around town. But this time was different.

At the station my father and uncles presented their call-up papers and were given tickets to board the train free of charge. Standing on the platform, I could see tears in my grandfather's eyes as they all shook hands and said goodbye. Silently my grandfather and I walked back to the horse and carriage. We didn't have to talk. On the way home we heard the whistle of the train approaching the station. 'God be with them!', my grandfather whispered as we trotted back towards town.

By the beginning of September things were getting tougher by the day – in particular food supplies were becoming more and more scarce. But I was still running around without a care in the world. Then the obvious happened on 1 September 1939.

I was in Market Square listening to the news on the restaurant radio when I heard a Polish military official announce that Germany had declared war on Poland. There was a strange silence throughout the town and everyone turned and walked away. That evening we heard air-raid sirens for the first time and the street lights didn't come on, even though there were no planes overhead. We boys thought it was fun to run about the town in the dark. We didn't realize the seriousness of it all.

The next day I met three of my friends in Market Square and we headed out in the direction of the railway station. We crossed the River Warta, over an old wooden bridge, going towards the new iron bridge built by the Germans. I knew it was built by the Germans because I used to see the German engineers outside Mr Trinkler's pastry shop.

A quarter of the way across the iron bridge we heard the heavy sound of aeroplanes and could see them flying low over our heads. We had never seen as many aeroplanes as this and we tried to count them. We lost count as they flew by in their hundreds. I noticed something dropping from one of the last planes that passed. Three large objects floated down towards the bridge we were standing on. We didn't know what was whistling through the sky, but they missed the bridge and dropped into the river right in front of us.

When we saw what was happening we panicked and ran for our lives back to town to tell everyone of the excitement we'd witnessed on the iron bridge. The air-raid sirens rang out louder and louder. When they stopped we told people what we'd seen. It wasn't until then that we learned that the mysterious flying objects were bombs. We were ignorant of the danger we would have been in had the bombs exploded on the bridge.

I went home to tell my mother about the planes. She was more interested in my hair and insisted that I go to the barber's straight away. He was cutting away around my ear when there was an enormous explosion. We both jumped with fright. Warm blood trickled down my face. 'You've cut my ear!', I yelled.

The barber stood stunned, his face white with fear. 'I caught a fright', he stammered. I was frightened too, but he had cut my ear and I was much more interested in my ear than the explosion. The bomb had landed somewhere out of town; no one knew exactly where.

By the end of the day the town was back to normal, except

that the street lights were still out and people were using torches to find their way around. All of us boys knew every inch of the town, even in the dark, and to us it was a lot of fun – we didn't have a care in the world. Late in the evening I finally went home and, as I walked through the door, my mother started shouting at me because she didn't know where I'd been.

'Don't you understand! There's a war going on!', she yelled. I explained about the planes and the bombs nearly hitting the bridge my friends and I had been on. She clasped her hands together and looked up at the ceiling. 'Thank God those big things never hit the bridge because you could all have been dead!', she whispered.

I began to realize what my mother was trying to tell me. She put my supper in front of me with a sigh of exasperation: 'Eat it all up and, when you finish, you're going to bed!'

In the middle of the night of 11–12 September, I was frightened out of my sleep by a knock on the window. I jumped out of bed and ran to wake my mother. Startled, she sat upright in bed and stared at the window: 'My God, it's your father!' She let him in. They hugged one another and my mother kept saying over and over: 'Thank God, thank God you all came back alive!' She turned on the lights and woke my brothers and sister. We sat at the table while my father told us what had happened to him and my uncles.

'At the time we left for Warsaw', he began, 'we arrived during the night at the main station and were met on the platform by military police. They called for the army reservists to report over to the right side of the platform. We were put into fours and marched a few miles outside Warsaw to a military base. When we got there nothing seemed to be organized; they didn't know what to do with us thousands of men. They had no uniforms, no boots, no weapons – not even gas masks.

'So they called us together and told us that we were dismissed and free to go home. We started to make our way to the main highway but, before we could reach the outskirts of Warsaw, there were heavy air raids. Waves of German bombers pounded the city day and night and the buildings were flattened right in front of our eyes. We somehow managed to get out of it and are lucky to be alive and able to sit here and tell the story.'

We all sat quietly and listened with great sadness to my father's story. Then he added: 'I know the war is not over and I expect the German army to march into Konin any day.'

My father was right. It happened on Thursday, 14 September 1939 on Rosh Hashanah, the Jewish New Year. At around seven o'clock in the morning my mother, having gone out for fresh milk, rushed into the house slamming the door behind her. We all jumped out of our beds frightened at the way Mother was screaming. The Germans had marched into Market Square.

I got dressed quickly and ran towards Market Square* to see what the Germans looked like. They were packing heavy artillery into the square. There were guns attached to large army trucks, motorbikes with machine guns mounted on the front of the side-cars and hundreds of army carriers speeding through 3 May Street on their way to Łódź and Warsaw. I ran home to tell my parents what was going on. I was upset to see a strange army invading our town so I decided to see what was going on from behind the curtains in our house.

---

*The heart of Konin's Jewish Quarter, which today is called *Plac Zamkowy*.

2 · Foretaste of Atrocities

Our house was on a corner near the market and its position was ideal for spying on the rest of the town. We had one big window facing the synagogue and two windows facing Market Square – I wouldn't miss a thing.

I saw lots of big cars without tops racing towards the synagogue. Tall Germans in black uniforms rushed into the synagogue waving pistols, firing single shots into the air. They were the murderous SS.

There was panic. I opened the window to hear what was going on. The SS were screaming *'Juden raus! Juden raus!'* The Germans stood either side of the big synagogue doors as the worshippers ran out into the street with their prayer shawls over their heads. The Germans were pushing them and beating them over the head with whips. I couldn't believe what I was seeing.

I was watching people I knew and lived with being beaten and harassed. I was worried that I might be in the same situation and I had to think of a way to survive. I watched with great sadness as the Germans cleared the synagogue of worshippers.

In the late afternoon, as it began to grow dark, I was still watching to see what the Germans would do next. I saw them call over a gang of Christian boys. I knew and played with most of these boys and was upset to see my old friends follow the SS. They went into the synagogue to help the Germans rip out the seats and carry them to Castle Square to throw them on to a pile about 20 metres from our window. They ran back and forth from the synagogue until they had built up a mountain out of the seats.

As if that wasn't enough, they ran back to the synagogue and returned carrying on their shoulders the beautifully decorated velvet-covered Torahs – the sacred Hebrew scrolls –

and tossed them on to the same pile. They raced backwards and forwards throwing the Torahs on to the pile until there were no more scrolls left. Next they ran out with prayer books, tossing them on the pile too. I became more and more angry as I watched my old friends co-operating with the Germans, destroying the synagogue. They burst out laughing as each prayer book was thrown. I wanted to smash my fist into their faces. I couldn't watch any longer and was moving to the door when my father stopped me: 'Where are you going?'

'I have to fight my old friends who're helping the Germans.'

'Don't be silly. Stay here until everything quietens down.' I went back to the window to see the humiliation the Germans were inflicting on the Jewish people of Konin.

I couldn't just sit and watch any longer so I found a way to sneak out of the house without my father noticing. As I reached the street I saw the rabbi walking towards me. He was surrounded by four SS men in black uniforms pushing him to make him walk more quickly. The rabbi tried to shuffle his old, tired feet but he couldn't run any faster. The SS men pushed through the spectators, finally reaching Market Square. They stopped in front of the pile of broken seats, scrolls and prayer books.

Even in all the confusion I noticed one of the SS officers lift his arm in the air giving a signal to another SS officer. Army trucks, carrying huge searchlights and movie cameras, sped into the square. The trucks formed a circle and after some discussion between the SS officers I heard a whistle.

Suddenly the searchlights blinded the crowd of onlookers. Two SS men appeared. One was holding a lady's hat, the other a bunch of long feathers. They put the hat on the rabbi and stuck the feathers into the brim of the old-fashioned hat, making him look foolish. Another SS man appeared with a torch and handed it to the rabbi. It took several tries with a match before the torch finally took light, revealing the fear in the face of the white-bearded rabbi. I wanted to cry for him as I watched his humiliation. The SS made him hop from one leg to another, while he was forced to put the torch to the sacred heap. In minutes the flames lit up the sky with all the colours of the rainbow. The SS enjoyed every moment of the spectacle. Worse still, the atrocity was filmed and photographed.

The commotion went on all evening. To me it seemed like ages, standing and watching, unable to do anything. After the filming stopped an SS officer approached the rabbi: 'You bloody old Jew! I'm going to give you a present! You know what that present is?' The rabbi shook his head to show that he didn't know. The SS officer reached for his holster and removed his pistol. The rabbi felt the cold gun against his head. He heard the SS man say: 'I am going to give you your life!' The rabbi could only stand with his head hanging, trembling with fear and disbelief that they were letting him live. He was in such a state of shock that he just stood there until two Jewish men led him home. Eventually the searchlights were turned off and the trucks made their way out of Castle Square.

When I got home I found my mother sitting by the window with a handkerchief in her hand wiping the tears that rolled down her face. The fire in Castle Square was so bright it lit up the inside of our house. My mother kept repeating: 'What is happening to the Jewish people in our town? We don't deserve this.' Watching the fire blazing into the sky in a host of colours my mother wept – and I wept with her. My father sat at the table resting his head on his arms.

We got up early the next morning and the first thing we did was run to the window to see if anything was going on in the streets. The fire in the square was still blazing. It burned for three days and nights. My father explained that the sacred Torah was parchment, made from animal skin, which was the reason for the brilliant colours coming from the fire.

As I watched from the window I could hear horses' hooves clattering down the cobblestone street towards the synagogue. A long convoy of carts loaded with bales of straw and hay followed. The German soldiers recruited the help of young Polish civilians to help unload the carts. They took off their jackets and began pushing wheelbarrows full of straw and hay up a wooden ramp into the synagogue. The Germans unhitched the horses and led them up the ramp into the synagogue.

Climbing through a window, I sneaked out of the house and rushed to the synagogue and in through the main entrance, where I hid by the door. The synagogue's beautiful crystal chandeliers were glowing with light. The Germans had turned the place of worship into a manure-filled stable. I was heart-broken.

One of the Germans looked up and caught me watching. I ran into the street. Even though I ran I wasn't frightened of them; I was thinking they could probably find me work with the horses. But on second thoughts, the one thing I wouldn't do was volunteer to work for the Germans – unless they forced me, or to save my life. I sat on the steps of the house opposite the synagogue and watched the Germans lead the horses up and down the platform as if the synagogue were a luxury hotel for horses.

There were German patrols throughout the town and they had set up headquarters in a 12-room house on 3 May Street. One morning I looked out of the window into the square and saw a crowd standing around the concrete billposter tower. I pushed my way through the crowd to get to the front and I came face to face with a big poster stuck to the tower which read:

Attention!
As from tomorrow morning no one must leave their homes before eight o'clock in the morning or after five o'clock in the evening. This is an order of the Commandant of the town of Konin. Whoever disobeys the orders of the Commandant will be shot without warning. This is an enforcement of a curfew by the Commandant.

And so it was. The next morning a young woman crossed the street to a tobacconist's shop and, having received no reply, walked away. As she was making her way back across the street a German patrol shouted '*Halt!*' He fired four shots and I saw her fall. Immediately all the German patrols in the surrounding streets came running over to where the woman lay. Within minutes a car arrived and out stepped a German officer. All the soldiers saluted him. The soldier who had shot the woman stepped forward, saluted and reported the incident.

9

'Very good, soldier. Orders are orders', said the officer, who got back into his car and sped away. The soldiers dispersed in an orderly fashion to resume their patrol duties. Half an hour later a Red Cross truck drove up, the dead woman's body was placed on a stretcher, covered with a blanket and the truck drove off quickly.

Conditions were deteriorating. Konin was coming to resemble a ghost town more and more. Schools and shops were closed and we were not allowed to go to the cinemas or any other public places. During the days I wandered around Market Square taking in everything I could see. It was like a play unfolding before my eyes.

The big market day, when people from the villages and countryside around Konin came to do their monthly shopping, was a few days later. The stall-holders sold everything you could imagine and it was so crowded I had to push my way through the crowds to reach my favourite stall with all the latest toys.

Suddenly shots rang out. People scattered in all directions, but I didn't run. When the police cleared the square the only people left were the stall-holders with their goods. From the other end of the square came a Mercedes Benz convertible heading towards the stall where I was standing. Out stepped five SS officers, in their black uniforms. They passed right in front of me and went straight to a Jewish stall-holder who sold ladies' underwear. They shouted at him and struck him on the face; they overturned his stall, scattering the underwear on to the ground. They put him in the open boot of the car and sped away. After a while people started coming back to finish their shopping.

There was commotion in the town now and everyone wanted to know what had happened to the stall-holder. A few days later I was in Market Square when I heard the sound of car horns. I ran to where the noise was coming from and saw three SS cars following one another into the town. The cars were moving slowly enough for me to walk beside the leading one.

Sitting on top of the bonnet, with his legs supporting his weight on the front bumper, was the underwear salesman.

They had put a cap on his head, back to front, to make him look ridiculous and he looked like he had been beaten up because he had cuts on his face and was bleeding. I noticed that lime had been smeared on his cuts to burn the wounds on his face. As if that wasn't enough, the SS made him carry a large billboard reading: 'I am a dirty Jewish blackmailer and I sell ladies' stockings and underwear to profit from poor Polish people.'

They drove all around town with the man on the bonnet of the car. The SS enjoyed every minute of the spectacle, as if the man represented all the Jewish people who lived in Konin. But that wasn't the case: it was just a propaganda exercise to humiliate the Jews by any means possible. After a two-hour show they drove back to their headquarters.

The next day, Thursday 21 September, the Germans began arresting influential people from the town as hostages; the reason given was that two German soldiers had been found shot dead. Another poster went up on the tower: 'Tomorrow morning at 11 o'clock the execution of two hostages will take place.'

The next morning just before 11 o'clock Liberty Square* was crowded; there were 300 or 400 people there. I pushed my way through the crowd to get to one of the two public water pumps in the square and climbed on top to have a good view of the spectacle. Over the heads of the crowd I saw the two condemned men being marched by six soldiers and one officer of the German army from the town prison to the square. The hostages came to a stop, facing the blank white wall of the old gymnasium. The crowd was silent. The men were told to turn and face the crowd.

One of the hostages, Mordechai Slodki, was a religious Jewish man of 70 who owned a fabric shop; I knew him well. The other was Aleksander Kurowski, a Polish Catholic who owned a posh restaurant near the main coach station. Everyone in town knew the restaurateur. You could always smell the food and hear the music from the four-piece band as you walked by his restaurant.

---

*Konin's main square, *Plac Wolnósci*.

A Catholic priest wearing a long mauve robe and a scarf around his neck approached the prisoners. He spoke first to the Jewish man. Then, with his Bible raised, he said a prayer with the Catholic man and made the sign of the cross. Then he turned and walked away. One of the Germans blindfolded the hostages.

The officer in charge ordered the firing squad to retreat 20 metres from the two men and take up their firing position. I was upset to watch what would be the first execution I would see. The officer in charge gave the order and the soldiers lifted their guns.

As the shots rang out I heard a horrific scream behind me: 'Holy Mary! O Lord! They've killed my father!' I was scared by the outburst and turned round to see Wiesław Kurowski, the restaurateur's son. He almost fainted as the two men fell into a single pool of blood. The firing squad swung their rifles over their shoulders at a command from their officer and marched away.

Some of the crowd moved towards the dead men. When I got close enough to see the bodies I couldn't believe my eyes: the men's arms and legs were still moving. Everyone was wiping tears from their faces as they passed the blindfolded corpses to show their last respects. Some made the sign of the cross.

By now it was only a few hours until curfew so I made my way home. My parents wanted to know where I had been since early morning. 'You look very sad. What have you been up to?', my mother asked. When I told them about the execution in the square and who the two men were, my father hung his head in sorrow. 'Good God!', my mother whispered and began to cry. She made an effort to control herself and gave me some soup and black bread, but I couldn't eat – I was much too upset.

I sat by the window and watched the German soldiers march through the town, six abreast, rifles hanging from their shoulders; the patrols were repeated every half-hour. All through the night I could hear the echo of jackboots on the cobblestone streets.

The town took on a deserted look and the few people who were walking around were not happy in these bizarre conditions. My mother and father were very suspicious of the Germans and I was furious because the SS murderers had taken away my freedom to move about the town in my usual way. I asked my father if there was somewhere we could run, but he said wherever we went it would be the same.

3 · *Cattle Truck to Ostrowiec*

On 30 November 1939, I heard army trucks speed past our window into the town square. SS soldiers ran through the streets banging on doors and pushing people into the street and on to trucks. 'My God, what are they doing to our people?', my mother cried.

We had just sat down to eat when we heard a pounding on our door. Three strapping SS men burst into our house, waving their pistols and screaming: 'You have five minutes to take whatever you can and get out of here!'

Weeping, Mother begged one of the men in German: 'Please give us five minutes longer so my children can finish their food.'

The man hesitated, looked at my father and asked: 'Who are you?'

'He is my husband', my mother replied quickly.

'Take your children and get out!'

My parents made us put on layers of clean clothes over the top of the ones we were wearing until we couldn't get any more on. 'Get out right now if you know what's good for you!', the German shrieked.

Mother managed to get some food together and that was all there was time for. No sooner was the door shut behind us than a soldier stuck a label with a skull and cross-bones on it reading: 'Whoever enters these premises will be shot without warning!'

We were pushed along by the SS to a waiting truck and hurried up a pair of makeshift steps. I saw lots of people I knew; people from our street and another street, one over from ours, were also being herded into the trucks. My mother was crying and Father was trying to comfort her: 'Whatever happens to us now is the will of God.' As he spoke these words the steps at the back of the truck were removed, the heavy doors slammed shut and the trucks began to move off.

Moments later we stopped. I jumped off to find myself being ushered into my old school. Here I saw lots of people I knew, including some of my school friends. We were being held here for deportation but they wouldn't tell us what our destination was.

We all lay on the floor with our belongings and discussed the situation. Many believed that if the SS could execute two innocent people, they were capable of anything. I thought to myself: 'I'm not going to be killed – I'm too young!'

The Gestapo continued to fill the school with people until late afternoon. Everything went quiet for a while. Then there was a commotion in the corridor when the SS returned. We were taken from the school, loaded into trucks with tarpaulin covers, then driven the short distance to the railway station. As we stopped I heard the big steps being placed against the truck and the shouting started again: '*Raus! Raus! Schnell! Schnell!*'

I ran among the crowd of bewildered people looking for my relatives. Someone I knew stopped me and asked who I was looking for. I told them I was looking for my grandparents and aunts and uncles from both sides of the family. He told me that the Jewish people had not yet all been brought to the station for deportation. When I told my mother she cried at the thought of being separated from the rest of the family. We wondered what would happen to them but there was nothing anyone could do apart from cry. We were completely surrounded by SS.

We were formed into groups of 70 and led through the main passenger terminal. There were many German civilians and high-ranking army officers milling around, waiting for trains to Berlin. The SS were a bit gentler with us in the terminal so as not to show the civilians what they were capable of.

As I walked through the terminal I could smell the rich cooking from the station restaurant. The Gestapo had forced out the previous Polish owners. I spotted the new German owners; their daughter was a good friend of my mother's sister, Aunt Golda. I hated the way the high-ranking Gestapo sat, laughing loudly, stuffing their faces with the excellent food and drink. Even more puzzling was the way my aunt's high school friend served them with a smiling face.

With the help of some Polish people, who had sided with the Germans, we were led at gunpoint to the station platform and across the railway tracks to a train made up of cattle trucks. I could hear people whispering that the train couldn't be for us. No one believed it could be until we were shoved with rifle butts up a ramp on to the filthy cattle train. Another group of people followed us, receiving the same treatment. The heavy rolling doors slammed shut behind us.

Everything went quiet. I lay on the floor in the dark listening to the express trains speeding through the station. All of a sudden there was a loud bang and, with a lot of whistles and blowing, the train moved away from the station to our unknown destination.

Soon we began to run out of the bread, sugar and milk my mother had tied in a tablecloth when the SS came for us. The train pulled into a station. We could hear Polish-speaking people. We banged on the door shouting for water, but we weren't let out of the train. Someone shouted back: 'There's no space to pass any water through.'

I had a bottle with me so I untied my trouser belt and tied it to the bottle. There was a narrow window in the side of the truck but I couldn't reach it. I stood on my father's shoulders and lowered the bottle through the window. Someone took it and a few moments later put the bottle, filled with water, back on to the belt. As I pulled the belt I heard someone shouting: 'Pull it up quick! There are guards coming!' I reeled in the bottle and it nearly reached the window when I heard a rifle shot and felt the bottle drop out of my hands. I jumped off my father's shoulders, uncertain whether to laugh or cry.

Soon after that the train jerked and we pulled out of the station. We travelled on and on, hardly knowing the difference between night and day. In the middle of a deep sleep in the corner of the cattle truck, I felt my mother pulling at me: 'Stand up, we're getting off the train.' The train had come to a halt. I could hear a commotion outside when the door rolled open and, for the first time in I don't know how long, we were breathing fresh air.

To our surprise there was an army field kitchen, run by the Swedish Red Cross, waiting for us. I could smell the aroma of boiling soup and ran to get some. But the Red Cross lady said I had to wait until everyone was off the train. I spotted a large basket with loaves of black bread cut into halves. It tempted me because I was so hungry, so I stole some. I ran over to my parents and gave them half. 'Srulek, where did you get this bread from?', my mother asked.

'I'm sorry, Mother, but I had to steal it.' I could see tears well in her eyes. 'Please don't cry, that's the only way we'll be able to carry on, otherwise we'll starve.'

My mother told Father I had stolen the bread. He called me over and said: 'Please don't ever do that again.'

I lost my temper: 'Don't tell me what to do!'

'Stop it, stop it!', my father screamed and he smacked me hard across the face. I turned and ran – but only in a circle to stand behind my father's back. I heard him apologize to Mother for losing his temper. I knew it wasn't the time for such childishness: very soon I would be forced to become a man.

Lines were formed and we were given large enamel bowls full of appetizing hot pasta soup. It must have been good soup because the guards kept going back for more. To us the Red Cross was a godsend. I think that without the Red Cross feeding us there would have been a few dead people on the train. There were a lot of older people among us who would not have survived without the soup and bread.

The guards and the SS officers showed us some respect and told us gently to get back on the train. Someone spread the word around that they were treating us so well because the Swedish officials were watching. The heavy doors of the cattle trucks were shut again and we were back in the dark. A few whistles later the train pulled away. We still didn't know our destination.

Through a tiny window in the cattle truck we could see day breaking. It was 3 December 1939. Everyone was waking up and wondering what would happen next. Suddenly the train slowed to a squeaky halt. One of the men in the train noticed the name on the railway station – Ostrowiec Świętokrzyski, an industrial town some 260 kilometres from Konin. Our family would spend the next 12 months here.

The train doors were rolled open and, to everyone's surprise, we heard people talking in Yiddish. I knew now there was at least hope of staying alive. I also noticed something I'd never seen before – Jewish policeman in long civilian overcoats wearing Polish ex-army belts and peaked hats with yellow bands. In one hand they carried a truncheon and on their right arm they wore a white armband with the Star of David.

There were queues of horses and carts, organized by the Gestapo and the Jewish police, to transport us all to the town's Jewish quarter. The Jewish police wanted to show their authority in front of the Gestapo by being aggressive as they put us in the carts. We were taken to the Jewish quarter several hundred at a time, travelling slowly over rough cobblestones, with the Gestapo leading the way.

In the Jewish quarter we were left in the hands of the Jewish police and a few minutes later, making our way through narrow streets, we arrived at a large synagogue. It had been stripped of its benches and converted into a hostel. On the floor were large square mats woven out of paper, stuffed with straw. But it looked welcoming compared with the conditions we'd experienced on the train so we made ourselves comfortable, two per mat.

After a little while the Jewish Council came and briefed us on what was to take place. Long tables were set up by the door and we were all issued with special coupons. These coupons were to be taken to another building and exchanged for ten-litre containers which were to be used in the communal kitchen to obtain soup and bread rations for all the family. We went to the kitchen every day to collect our rations.

One day the Jewish Council told us we had been allocated a two-bedroom house which we had to share with another family. My mother was not happy about this, but Father told her we had no option. We were, however, on a list to be allocated, in a few weeks' time, one of the new prefabricated barracks which had two bedrooms and a kitchen. This made Mother a little happier. In the meantime she picked out a family we knew from Konin to share the house. We registered with the Jewish Council and moved in straight away.

*

1. The author's Uncle Bernard, owner of a car hire business,
Konin 1927.

2. The author's mother Helena in the 1930s.

3. Corner of the street (left) where the author's house stood before it was demolished by the Nazis.

4. The iron bridge in Konin bombed by the Germans in September 1939, when the author and Polish friends narrowly missed being hit.

5. Konin Town Hall.

6. Konin County Hall, used by the Nazis for offices and accommodation.

7. Execution of two hostages, a Christian and a Jew, in Konin on 22 September 1939.

4

8. Aunt Golda (centre) with Polish high school friends. She and her brother Revuz were murdered by Gestapo officers in front of the author.

9. Prisoners being transported from camp to camp.

10. Prisoners forced to pose for the photograph by SS Guards, presumably for propaganda.

11. A death march of concentration camp prisoners.

12. This is the place in The Kazimierz Forest where some of the Konin Survivors in 1945 put up a memorial plaque for the victims who were executed there in 1941.

13. The author in 1946 after disposing of his
Polish army uniform.

I made friends with a boy who lived across the road from us whose name was Gerhard Werner. I could never make out why he spoke a mixture of German and Yiddish and not just Yiddish or Polish.

One day Gerhard invited me to his house and introduced me to his mother. His mother, who spoke only German, asked me to stay and have something to eat. In the next room I noticed lots of men playing cards. There was a knock at the door and Gerhard's father rushed to answer it. At the door were four SS officers, so tall their heads almost touched the ceiling. As I was running out through the back door I heard Gerhard greet the men: 'Uncles, uncles!'. I was frightened when I saw the black SS uniforms so I ran across the street and watched from my front doorstep. There was an SS man in a Mercedes Benz convertible parked in front of the house reading some documents. I suppose it was to see who was to be executed next.

An hour or so later the SS men came out of the house followed by the Werner family. The men got into the car and sped away while the Werners waved goodbye. Gerhard came across the street to me and I asked him about the SS men.

'They are my uncles', he said.

'How can they be your uncles if you are Jewish and they are German SS?'

'When my father was a young boy he emigrated to Germany', Gerhard answered. He stopped and ran into the street shouting 'Grandfather! Grandfather!'. The only people I could see in the street were an old religious Jewish man with a long beard, holding on to a young man's arm. Gerhard ran up to the old man and gave him a hug.

When he came back I said to him: 'I don't understand. How can you be related to the Jewish man and at the same time have uncles who are SS officers?'

'When my father emigrated to Germany in the 1920s he was looking for work but couldn't find any. He boarded a train for Paris. A young woman served him dinner in the restaurant carriage and he asked her if there were any jobs going. She told him she would ask her father and that's how my parents met. One year later they got married in Munich. So now you can understand: I am half-Jewish and half-German.'

I never doubted Gerhard's truthfulness. But I wanted to know why they left Munich to come to Poland. 'One day, when the Gestapo had begun persecuting the Jews', he continued, 'there was a knock on our door. It was the Gestapo. They interrogated my parents, about my mother being married to a Jew. They said German law did not permit mixed marriages, especially to Jews. They told my mother she could stay in the homeland with me and my two sisters only if she divorced my father. They gave them two days to decide. The next day my parents locked the house, boarded a train and crossed the German–Polish border. That's how we got to Ostrowiec to be with my father's family.'

The next day Mrs Werner sent Gerhard over with two white loaves of bread and a large stick of chicory to make coffee. My mother thought Mrs Werner was a wonderful woman.

One morning posters were put up around the Jewish quarter. 'Attention! In three days' time a hanging will take place in Market Square. Residents of Ostrowiec are invited to come and see what happens to hostages who support partisans in assassinating a high-ranking German SS man.'

Soon the square was busy with SS soldiers and trucks carrying timber. I was puzzled about the timber so I returned the next morning to see what was going on. There were ten carpenters, Polish and Jewish, who were forced to build gallows. Their job was completed by the evening.

The following morning the Gestapo drove through the ghetto ordering everyone into Market Square. I was the first to run out of the house, but there was already a small crowd waiting on the pavement in the square. More and more people soon gathered and not long after the Gestapo rushed into the square, stopping near the gallows. Four men in masks got out of a car and turned to face the crowd. I recognized one of the men because I had a lot of connections with his family. The Gestapo showed the masked men how to put the ropes on the gallows. The men climbed up and down until they had hung 30 ropes, each with a loop on one end. When the gallows were prepared, one wooden ladder and one high stool remained.

I looked down the road leading to the prison and watched the group of hostages, surrounded by SS men, march into the square and stop in front of the gallows. Four black-uniformed SS officers got together for a quick consultation. A moment later one of the SS men took a hostage, led him up to the gallows and made him climb up on to the stool. With a white face and trembling knees the hostage stood facing the crowd as the SS man read from his clipboard. The Polish man was accused of the assassination of a high-ranking German SS officer.

One of the masked men climbed on to the gallows and put the loop of one of the ropes around the hostage's neck. An SS man kicked the stool from underneath his feet and the man dropped, hanging by his neck with his hands tied behind his back, twisting round and round. This continued until all 29 men were hanged and one empty rope remained.

The Gestapo left and the crowds dispersed, but I went up to the gallows to get a closer look at the hanging men's faces. As I stood looking at the dead men, a horse and cart drove underneath the gallows. Four SS men — with smudged black faces to conceal their identity – cut down the hostages and placed them in the cart. The bodies of the hostages were covered with straw and taken away. No one ever knew where they were buried.

The next day I learned that the man intended for the thirtieth rope was a Polish doctor. He had committed suicide in his prison cell.

A few days later my friend Gerhard and his mother came to our house with a big box. Mrs Werner placed the box on the table and said: 'My dear friends, I have brought this food to you and I have more. Tomorrow morning my children and I are catching a train to Munich to go home to our family in Germany.'

I could see the tears in her eyes as she hugged my mother. 'I wish you could take your family and get away from this town because things are going to get very bad here.'

My mother was unable to make her understand that we couldn't run anywhere because we were not in the same position: she was German and we were Jews. We couldn't travel without a German permit and not many Jews could get one. My father said the Werners had no problem in getting permits: her brothers who were SS probably gave them unrestricted travel documents.

The next morning I looked across the street and watched the Werner family load their cases on to a horse and cart and slowly pull away. We all waved goodbye and that was the last time I saw my friend Gerhard and his family.

4 · Put to Work by the Gestapo

About a week later two Jewish policeman brought orders for us to move to a new place the following morning. We were also to register with the main central committee for forced labour and report the next day for work.

My father was selected to work at the German horse stables and I was given work at the Gestapo headquarters. That evening my father arrived home with a sack of black bread. 'When we got to the stables', he began, 'the *Arbeitsdienstführer* asked which of us were familiar with horses. I said I was and he made me the foreman over the other men.

'He counted five men to go in four different trucks to the goods station. When we got there we found a train loaded with bales of straw and hay. We loaded the trucks and went back to the stables. We unloaded the hay and made a second trip to the train. We unloaded the second load, then cleaned out the stables and fed the horses.

'The sergeant told us he was going to make a special request to the Jewish Council for us to come back to work at the stables. He said we had done a good job, especially me, and he asked my name. When I told him, he asked if I was a German Jew, but I told him I was a Polish Jew.

'He had a store room at the back of his office full of rations and he told us to take two loaves of bread each. Then we loaded up a truck and they brought us back to the Jewish quarter.'

In the community hall at the Jewish Council headquarters I was selected along with 14 other men by a Gestapo man named Bruno. The Jewish chief told us to go out to the front gate and form ourselves into threes. Bruno had a large Alsatian that ran between our legs sniffing our feet.

We marched along the road, with the dog leading the way, to the Gestapo headquarters. About a mile and a half outside town we came to a big house and marched through a gate. We'd been standing in the square about 20 minutes when five Gestapo officers came out of the building. Bruno introduced them to us: 'This is our chief, Herr Langer. This is Herr Wagner and Herr Ostman, and this is Herr Peters. You know my name so let me hear it!' We all shouted: 'Herr Bruno!'

'And don't forget it!', he threatened. They made us shout *'Heil Hitler!'* until they were satisfied we'd shouted loud enough. The SS men all had smiles on their faces. 'You're here to work', Bruno shouted. 'I will allocate the work to you. If you want to live, you'll do a good job.'

Langer interrupted. 'You', pointing at me, 'do you understand horses?'

'Ja wohl, Herr Langer', I said.

'Come with me then.' I followed him to a stable. When he opened the door there was a grey horse identical to one of my grandfather's horses. Everything about the family I'd left behind flashed through my mind.

The Gestapo chief told me: 'I want the horse to be very clean and when you've finished you come and tell me.'

I began combing the horse, but he became restless. I tried telling him to stand still, but he wouldn't take any notice. I thought maybe the horse only understood German so I said to him: *'Still halten!'* The horse obeyed my command and I groomed him until he was very clean. I even painted his hooves with black paint.

I tied the horse to a post near the stable. I was still sweating but I had to report to the chief. I knocked on the door of the headquarters. The door opened violently and I was standing in front of Gestapo officer Wagner. He was wearing black braces over his white shirt and he had a pistol in his hand.

'What's your problem?', he snarled.

'There is no problem, sir. I would like to tell Herr Langer that I've finished cleaning his horse.'

'One moment!' He spoke to me so arrogantly that I thought he was going to put the pistol to my head and pull the trigger. To a Gestapo officer, shooting somebody was like lighting a cigarette.

I took the horse and paraded up and down while waiting for the Gestapo chief. When the chief arrived he watched me walk the horse for a while then said: 'You have done a good job. Take the horse and tie it up outside the stable.' He put his hand out for the horse to lick and patted its clean neck. 'Now the stable needs cleaning. But come with me.' I followed him across the yard. We stopped outside two big gates and they opened to reveal a powerful German motorbike, covered in grease. 'I want you to make a clean job of this machine.'

'Yes, Herr Langer.' And he left me to it. But he hadn't left me anything to clean it with so I had to think quickly. I took off one of my woollen socks and unscrewed the petrol cap on the bike. I dipped my sock in the petrol and started cleaning the filthy engine. I even had to scrape off the grime with my fingernails.

I was looking out for the rest of the men but I couldn't see anybody. I could hear sawing in the basement of the headquarters building, so I knew the men had been put to work cutting logs. I cleaned the bike while keeping an eye on the entrance to the yard, watching the SS coming and going.

The SS chief walked into the yard followed by an old Jewish man whom he had brought to clean out the stable. I watched from across the yard and took pity on the old man; I could tell he was very nervous. The chief left him to get on with the job. I had finished cleaning the chief's motorbike and ran across the yard. 'Herr Langer, I've finished cleaning your bike.' He looked at the bike but didn't say anything right away.

'This is very good, it's very clean', he said at last. As I stood with the chief I saw that the old man hadn't started his task. He was clearly frightened of the horse. I asked Herr Langer if he would let me help the old man clean out the stable. I knew that when the chief came back and the job wasn't done he would shoot the old man. 'I think you like my horse', Herr Langer said.

I went in to the stable and brought the horse out and tied it to a post. I gave the old man a broom and I found an old pitch fork. 'If you hear someone coming start sweeping the floor', I told him. I was lucky enough to find an old wheelbarrow to put the stable manure in and I wheeled it around the back to a field.

When I was confident the stable was clean enough for the Gestapo chief, I led the horse in while the old man waited outside. I went across the yard and knocked on the chief's door. Again, someone opened the door abruptly. I was once again standing in front of one of the worst killers in the SS, Officer Wagner. 'What do you want?'

'Herr Langer told me when I finished cleaning the stable I should report to him.'

'Wait here', he said, slamming the door in my face. After a few minutes the chief appeared. He went into the stable and looked around. He had a grin on his face. It was very unusual for a Gestapo chief to have a grin on his face. He couldn't believe what a clean job we'd done.

'Come with me.' We followed him to the headquarters building. 'You wait here till I come back. You understand?'

'Yes, sir.'

A big Mercedes Benz convertible drove up to the headquarters door with six Gestapo officers, who were laughing and joking as though drunk. They knocked on the office door. The old man and I stepped aside. The door opened and I heard the clicking of heels and '*Heil Hitler!*' salutes. The chief saluted back with one hand and with the other held a big paper bag which he handed over to the old man. 'I want you to come back tomorrow.'

'Yes, sir', I said. 'Sir, we can't go through the streets in case we're stopped by a patrol. Sir, would you please issue us with a pass?' He went back into his office and came back with another paper bag and gave it to me. He gave us each a pass and we walked out through the gate, past an SS guard. When I looked at my pass there was a big black stamp on it and it was signed by the chief himself.

It was getting dark as we made our way home. As we walked with the paper bags we saw an SS patrol. It was the first time we had seen an SS patrol in the town but I wasn't worried because we had the best passes it was possible to have. I knew we were going to be stopped, especially carrying two paper bags over our shoulders. One of them shouted: '*Halt!* What have you got in those paper bags?'

'I don't know', I answered.

'Why don't you know?'

'These bags were given to us by the chief of the Gestapo, Herr Langer. We didn't want to look inside them until we got home.'

'Empty the bags on to the pavement!', he shouted. I was curious to see what came out of my bag: tins of preserved meat and two large loaves of black bread. I was happy with what the Gestapo chief had given us but I was watching to see what they were going to do with the old man's bag. He was very frightened when they told him to empty his bag. I pulled the pass from my pocket and told the old man to show his pass as well. The SS man looked at them, then took them to his sergeant while the other soldiers stood around us, rifles at the ready.

After they had looked at the passes, they told us to pick up all the things on the pavement and go home. I walked the old man home and outside his street door he said to me: 'I will never forget what you have done for me.'

'Don't worry, we're not going back tomorrow to the Gestapo headquarters because the Jewish Council will send a different group of people to work for the Gestapo.' I saw tears in the old man's eyes. 'Be well', I said and walked on with my paper bag.

When I told my family about my day I said to my mother: 'I can't understand why a Gestapo chief should give two Jewish people all that food to take home. But not only that, the two passes he wrote out, stamped with the SS insignia, said more than words. Even the patrol were impressed because they saw it was signed by the chief. You know what I'm thinking? Maybe he was so good to me because I look a bit like his son.'

The chief lived with his family in a large house near the church. I used to see them being picked up every day by a chauffeur-driven car that had triangular black flags on each side of the wings. I did look a bit like his son, the difference being that his son wore a Hitler Youth uniform.

It is true that Langer gave me food and looked after me but that didn't make him an angel. No one on this earth was as merciless as the Gestapo. They never hesitated to take a pistol from their holster and put it to the back of someone's head and pull the trigger. Every day blood was spilled on the roads and the pavements. This is how Jewish people had to live, not knowing from day to day what would happen next.

*

Ostrowiec was crowded with SS troops, taking their position in the town's Market Square. Not many people would walk through the square. But I wasn't frightened to walk among the SS troops because I was starving. I spoke reasonable German and began begging for food.

Once I saw an SS soldier trying to unload boxes of tinned meat off the back of a truck. 'Please, sir', I asked. 'Would you help me, sir, with some cans of meat and bread? I'm very hungry.'

'You jump up on my truck and hand me down some of the boxes and I'll give you some food', he replied.

I couldn't get on the truck fast enough. When the truck was unloaded the soldier pointed to white sacks filled with round bread and said: 'Hand them to me.' Then he told me to wait by the truck and he walked away. He returned in an army jeep and I helped him load the jeep with the meat and bread. The soldier packed a white sack with cans of meat and loaves of bread and handed it to me. I thanked him and swung the bag over my shoulder.

On my way home I ran into four of my Polish friends. 'What are you doing here?'

'We're very hungry and thought maybe the Germans would give us some food', they answered.

'It's not as easy as you think', I said, 'because you don't speak German and the SS soldiers don't speak Polish. So you won't get anything from them unless I help you. I tell you what we'll do. I'll take two of you with me, but two of you must stay behind and hold my sack. Go to the corner of Market Square and wait for us. I don't want you to get any ideas about going off with my sack. If you do I'm not going to help you get any food.'

They swore they would wait for us. We walked further into Market Square. My Polish friends were very nervous, but I had already had experience of the SS murderers. They didn't worry me all that much, as long as I could get as much food as possible to take home to my family.

There was laughter coming from one of the SS trucks. 'Let's ask the happy lot in that truck', I said. 'But I warn you, I don't trust them. When we ask for food I'm going to ask them very politely in case they're drunk and start shooting. If they do, you'll have to run for your life in between the trucks.'

Their faces were white with fear. I approached the truck and asked politely in German: 'Could you spare us some food?' I had to ask several times until one of the soldiers answered.

'How did you learn to speak such good German?'

'My family is *Volksdeutsche*', I lied.

He believed me and asked another soldier in the truck if they could give me something. The two of them brought us four long loaves of bread and four German salami sausages. I thanked him repeatedly and ran off to meet the other two boys.

They were in heaven when they saw what we had obtained, but I made them share it equally. Then I took my sack and made my way home.

Several days later SS soldiers began constructing barbed-wire barricades on the main road to Ostrowiec. No one could get in or out of the Jewish quarter without a permit. Signs were put up announcing that anyone passing the wire boundaries without authorization would be shot without warning. There were posters everywhere saying that Jews must not be found in the streets before eight in the morning or after five in the evening. What's more, every Jew, young or old, must wear at all times an armband on their right arm, marked with the Star of David.

Some of the younger people in the Jewish quarter didn't take any notice and tried to pass the boundaries. They were fired on and killed. As for me, I don't know why but I was never frightened of anything because I never believed I could be killed.

One day I took off my armband and, posing as a Polish Christian boy, tried to cross the barbed-wire boundaries. I heard a rifle shot and ran up the hill towards the Catholic church. When I looked around, SS soldiers were examining a dead body.

I eventually found a way to pass the boundaries which the Germans never discovered. The barriers represented the division between the Polish Christian people and the Jews. Three-quarters of the town was occupied by Poles and one-quarter by the Jews. In the Jewish quarter there wasn't much to do and not much food around. That is why I was so anxious to cross the barrier, where there was no shortage of food and no restrictions on movement.

One morning I crossed the forbidden border my secret way and walked down the high street. I passed by the German police station and noticed a big horse and cart with two German soldiers unloading woven baskets filled with bread and small barrels of butter. I watched the soldiers carry the food into the police station. About 15 minutes later they were back for another load.

The minute they walked through the door and disappeared for the second time, I sprinted across the road and helped myself to what I could carry. I picked up two loaves of bread and one barrel of butter and then ran back across the road to mingle with the Polish people.

I made my way home safely with the food, but I didn't tell my parents how I'd obtained it. If I had, there would have been a lot of screaming from my mother about how I'd risked my life. We all enjoyed the food while I planned to go back the next day.

Suddenly we heard shooting in the street. There was panic. The Germans had stepped up their day-to-day street executions. When the shooting stopped I went outside and saw people lying in pools of blood. They had been dragged outside their own doors and shot.

5 · Family Deported to Treblinka

One morning at the end of 1940 the Germans made an announcement that everybody in the Jewish quarter must be in the city square by 11 o'clock. Anybody found in their homes after this time would be shot. We packed what we could and, as we were ready to leave, my father said: 'This time I think it's for good. But let's hope not.' By now the rumours of death camps had penetrated the walls of the Jewish quarter and no one could be sure what would happen next.

'I've had enough of hoping', I said. 'This time I'm going to take a chance and do things my own way.' My brother Karol agreed and wanted to come with me.

'Don't take any chances', my mother pleaded. 'They'll kill you!' But I wasn't listening to my mother. My mind was made up.

Father looked at me and said: 'If you want to do things your own way, son, try to get away from here and save yourselves. I know we are going to die.'

'If they kill you and I live through this I will get my revenge.' Those are the last words I ever spoke to my parents and younger brother and sister.

Weeping, my mother said that God should help both of us and that we should look after one another. They kissed us goodbye for the last time and we ran off, with tears streaming down our cheeks. Karol was 12 and I was 13.

We ran towards the high street in the direction of the main railway station. We heard shouts and shooting and adults and children screaming. An Estonian execution squad was shooting people indiscriminately in the streets and through the windows of their houses. Entire families were being dragged into the street and shots were being fired at random into crowds of people, murdering men, women and children without mercy.

We ran into a huge doorway, to get out of sight of the execution squad. The gate was locked and the door had two large crosses daubed on it in white paint to distinguish the Christian inhabitants from the Jewish ones. We heard shouting: 'Stay where you are!' We ran to another gate and forced it open, hearing gun shots behind us. When I looked back I saw two bullet holes on the gate door. They'd missed us by inches.

We had no option but to keep running, from garden to garden, round the backs of houses and over fences, until we reached the big church on top of the hill. We were resting on the grass in front of the church when we heard rifle shots. Coming round the bend, in the middle of the road, were the SS, leading people from the Jewish quarter to the town's main railway station. The people were surrounded by SS soldiers with guns at the ready. From time to time the soldiers ran between the tormented people, striking them with their rifle butts.

Karol and I watched with tears in our eyes but we had to keep running to reach the station before the SS arrived. We ran down the hill to the station and were shocked by the number of Polish people standing watching the groups of Jews being marched in by the execution squad and loaded on to a long goods train.

I saw another group of people being hurried by the SS, shouting '*Schnell! Schnell!*' To my horror I spotted my mother holding my sister's hand and looking extremely distressed. Then I saw my father following, holding my brother's hand. I followed behind the barrier to see where they were going, then we saw them being hurried on to the platform bridge and pushed into a wagon.

Karol began weeping and said to me: 'I want to go on the train with Mother and Father and my brother and sister.' Both of us wept.

An SS soldier holding a clipboard was counting the people being loaded into each wagon. Then he slammed the big sliding door closed and went to the side of the wagon where there was a blackboard attached and, with a white stick and chalk, he wrote in large letters: 'TREBLINKA'. I knew I would never see my family again – Treblinka was an extermination camp.

We stood in front of the crowd of Polish people and watched the engine belching out smoke and steam. A middle-aged couple standing next to me saw Karol and me crying. 'This is no place for two young boys, to stand here and watch all this. Why don't you go home?', said the woman. I wondered if she knew we didn't have a home to go to.

The SS guards and their Alsatian dogs stood grouped together waiting for the SS chief to give the signal for the train to move off. He lifted his hand, the whistles sounded, the wheels started spinning on the railway tracks and the train started to move. The train, carrying my family, vanished into a thick black smoke.

The crowd at the station moved away talking among themselves, sympathizing with the people on the train. But they had homes and families to go back to. The two of us were walking away, sobbing with the pain in our hearts. I was holding Karol around the shoulders. We walked away like two lost sheep with nowhere to go.

I decided we should make our way back home the same way we had come. So we went back to the church, looking down into the streets. It was quiet and deserted but we still went through the back gardens and fences to get to our home. We couldn't walk through the streets because we could still hear rifle shots.

Back at the house we sobbed again. Karol was sitting on one bed and I was on the other, sobbing in silence with our faces in our hands, grieving for our family because deep down in our hearts we knew where they had gone – along the road of no return. I said to Karol: 'Let's see if we can find Mother's handbag, I know she kept all the family photographs in it.' We searched in vain. She had taken all the little possessions with her and we were left without a single memento of our family.

'Let's go down the street and see where we can go from here.' As we walked through the gate we saw an Estonian execution squad, with a German SS officer in command, walking towards us. We couldn't run back because they were too close. Had we run we would certainly have been shot dead. The SS officer shouted '*Halt!*' We stopped still, not to give them any excuse to shoot us. They walked seven abreast, covering the whole road, their rifles at the ready. They encircled us and one of the Estonians said to the others in Russian: 'I think they're Jews.' They weren't sure and one answered: 'They don't look like Jews.' The German SS came over and said to the Estonian officer in broken Russian: 'Open his shirt and see if they're wearing anything round their necks.'

The Estonian came towards me, smelling of vodka, and opened my shirt. To the amazement of the executioners he saw around my neck a crucifix hanging on a shoelace which I had once been given by a Polish friend. I always carried it with me, in my pocket, and my brother carried a St Christopher. But we had hung them around our necks at the right time. I believe that, as a Jew, Jesus Christ saved my life and St Christopher saved my brother's life.

'Go home!', shouted the German SS man when he saw the Christian icons, but we stood there making out we didn't understand until one of the Estonians said in Polish: 'Go home.' We slipped into the front garden of a house, pretending we lived there, then ran through the back of the house looking for an escape route. We continued to hear rifle fire very close to us in the streets.

We jumped from one roof-top to another until we came to a low house at the edge of the restricted area of the city. We waited on the roof until dusk, but then I could no longer stand hearing shot after shot being fired at innocent people. I knew that if we could get to the other side of the barbed-wire barricade we would be safe, for a while at least.

When I looked down into the street I said to Karol: 'Look at the lamppost. See all those horses tied up. I'm going to get one of them and make a run for it.'

'Me too', Karol said.

'No. Look down there, there are six or eight SS guards with rifles hanging from their shoulders, guarding the entry to the main road to the city.' There was only one way to run and that was past the guards. 'You know what will happen – they're going to fire at me. So listen to me and remember: if that happens, you make a run for it to the house across the road. From there make your way to Aunt Golda. You know where she lives?'

'Yes.'

'Don't forget. Be careful – one of us has got to make it!' I saw tears in his eyes. I gave him a hug and said: 'Don't worry about me. When I start riding, make sure you have a clear run without being shot and make it to Aunt Golda and stay there till I come back. Ready? The minute I'm between the horses, run across the road without being seen, then you'll be safe. You've got to make it!'

I jumped down from the low roof, crept towards the horses, untied one of them, put one foot in the stirrup and hit the horse under the belly. It took off with such force that sparks were coming out from underneath its shoes as it galloped past the SS guards.

I could feel my heart beating as though it would burst out of my chest. I lowered myself to one side of the horse so I wouldn't be seen, holding on tight to the saddle. The SS guards tried to stop the horse, waving their arms in the air, thinking it was running away. One of them spotted me hanging on the side of the horse and began firing. I held on tight and galloped frantically towards the forest.

6 · With the Polish Partisans

The gunfire behind me began to fade and the further I went the more secure I felt. I rode faster and faster through the fields. As I approached the forest, I saw rifle fire coming out of the forest shooting past me in the direction of the SS. When I realized the shooting wasn't meant for me I jumped off the frightened horse and let it run loose. Standing at the edge of the forest I watched my horse join the retreating SS soldiers.

I wandered through the forest eating old dried-out berries. The sound of dry twigs breaking interrupted me and I hid behind an oak tree, peering from behind to see who was in the forest. I thought the SS had come searching for me, but I saw four civilian men. One of them shouted: 'Stop where you are and put your hands up!'

Two of the men escorted me to a house deep in the forest. 'I want to see the captain', one of them said to a man guarding the house.

'Hold on.' And he disappeared into the house for a minute.

I was taken inside and made to sit on an old wooden chest in the corner of the room. A tall man with blond hair, wearing riding boots and with a gun around his waist, came down the stairs. He stared at me and told the other two men to leave. 'What's your name?', he asked.

'My name is Srulek Hahn.'

'You're Jewish!'

'Yes. If I wasn't Jewish I wouldn't have had to run for my life!' By the way he said 'You're Jewish!' I didn't know whether to trust him or to run away again as soon as I got the opportunity. However, I had no option, for the time being, and nowhere to go. My life was in his hands; after all some of his men had already saved my life.

'Now, tell me how old you are.'

'I am 15, going on for 16.' In fact, I was only 13 but I had to

tell him a lie because I was worried in case he sent me away
for being too young.

When I had told him everything he wanted to know he
said: 'I'm sorry about your family. But don't worry. Do you
know where you are?'

'No.'

'This is the Polish partisan underground army. As you're
Jewish, do you speak German?' He smiled when I said I did.
'Good. I will have a very important mission for you soon.'

He turned towards the stairs and called for Maria. I saw a
girl in her mid-twenties, also wearing leather boots and a gun
around her waist, walk down the stairs. She looked a bit out
of place to me; I could tell she was a city girl.

'Show the young man where he can stay', said the captain,
whose name was Bronowski.

Maria placed her arm around my shoulders and we walked
out behind the old house to a large barn full of straw. 'Make
yourself comfortable', she said. 'Do you want anything to
eat?'

'I wouldn't mind something', I said, overwhelmed at the
situation I'd found myself in. When Maria went to get coffee
and bread the other men hidden in the straw called out:
'What's your name?'

'I'm Jewish and my name is Srulek.' I told them I was
Jewish because I would have known right away if they were
anti-Semitic by their remarks and their behaviour towards me.
But they accepted me as a good friend.

Two of the men said the way I had got to the forest was
heroic. 'We all admire you', one man said. 'And we think the
captain will have a lot of use for a Jewish boy like you,
especially since you understand German.'

'I'm not very happy that I understand German because I
hate what I've seen, the way they were spilling the blood of
innocent people in the streets of Ostrowiec.' After I had told
them about the Jewish quarter there was silence in the barn.

Some time later Maria called to me: 'Srulek, come with me.' I
followed her across the farmyard to the house. She led me to
a large room where all the men stood around the captain, who
was sitting behind an old table in the centre of the room.

'Come forward', the captain ordered. I was told to kneel down as he put a Bible in front of me. 'Place your left hand on it and raise two fingers of your right hand.' Looking around the room, he continued: 'You are witnesses today to Srulek swearing that he will be a good, true fighter for the freedom of our country.' Raising two fingers on his right hand he said: 'Repeat after me: "I swear to give my life and fight to the last moment for the freedom of my country against the German Nazis. Amen."'

After I had repeated the oath he placed a German automatic gun around my waist. 'Good luck. Now you're all dismissed.' Before I could get to the door the captain called me back: 'Do you know how to use a gun?'

'No', I said, ashamed.

He laughed and said: 'Come outside with me.' He instructed one of the guards to teach me how to use a gun properly, because I was the youngest one there. I sat on a bench with the guard and he showed me how to load and unload the gun. He said I did it perfectly.

The guard took me to the back of the house and showed me a concealed door which led to a staircase. At the bottom of the stairs I saw a large underground cellar set up with tables and benches. A man in one corner of the room, with earphones on his head, was operating a wireless set. In another corner a man was setting letters on a hand printing press.

On the floor was a door leading to yet another cellar. The man I was with said to me: 'This is an emergency underground cellar. If we ever got surrounded, we would come down here.' Then we walked into the forest and the man showed me around and how far I could go out.

Back at the house the other men were sitting around in small groups. Some were playing cards, others were cleaning their rifles and one man was playing a harmonica. I sat with the group cleaning their guns and asked one of them to show me how to use his rifle. He told me to lay on the ground, flat on my stomach, in the firing position. I tried it a few times and the man said I was a quick learner. Someone called us all into the captain's room. We all filed through at once.

The captain chose 13 men, including me, for a very

important mission. He took a map from the drawer in the table and pointed to a prison marked on it. 'In there are about 50 hostages who must be released. This is an order from headquarters. You men will have to be dressed in German uniforms which will be delivered in about half an hour.'

When the uniforms arrived we were shown the map of the Ostrowiec prison again. It was a prison now, but before the war it had been a Polish police station. There were many cells in the cellars beneath the building, and they could hold a large number of prisoners. I felt relieved because I knew the police station wasn't heavily guarded. I told the captain there was one sentry box in front of the big gates. Inside the prison was a German prison officer and a Polish prison warden working for the Germans: 'He's got a glass eye and his name's Ludwik.'

'You have more information than I do', said the captain.

'Don't forget I've been there before – I lived in a house at the back of the prison yard with my family and I would watch what was going on behind the prison fence every day.'

'Tomorrow', the captain said, 'you're going to march to the prison station and get all the prisoners out. And you' – he pointed at me – 'you can command the group of 12 uniformed men. I know you will all be protecting one another and you will all come back alive. Good luck!'

The following day, as we walked to the edge of the forest towards the main road leading to Ostrowiec, I practised my German so the men could understand me when it came to the real thing. An hour into the walk I remembered I was supposed to have picked up documents to be handed over to the German commandant of the prison who would release the prisoners. One of the other men had been given the papers and told by the captain to give them to me when we reached the prison.

When we got to the prison I told the guards to open the gates and we marched into the prison yard. *'Abteilung halt!'*, I shouted. The man with the papers came over to me, clicked his heels and with a *'Heil Hitler!'* salute handed me the orders. I handed the papers to the guard, also with a *'Heil Hitler!'* salute, and clicked my heels. 'These papers contain my orders.'

He took the papers and walked through the narrow gate into the prison yard to see his commandant. Soon he opened the main prison gates. We marched in and the prison warden opened the cell doors. The warden and I both shouted to the prisoners: '*Raus! Raus!*' We pushed and shoved them to make it look real.

As we marched the prisoners along the street I heard them shout to each other: 'Now they're going to shoot us!' I whispered: 'You're not going to be shot. You're going to fight for freedom. We aren't murderers. We're the Polish partisan movement.' We lined the prisoners up in threes, I saluted '*Heil Hitler!*' and we marched off towards the forest. We walked and walked. No one complained: they were all glad to be alive.

A couple of days later another man and myself were placed on guard duty at the outskirts of the forest. As we lay, hidden behind bushes, my friend spotted four German soldiers on horseback. When I looked closer I saw the Germans had a civilian walking in front of them. As they neared the edge of the forest my friend became nervous and wanted to shoot. I pushed his rifle down towards the ground: 'Let's make sure who the civilian is before we fire.'

As they came closer my friend became impatient and started to shoot. The Germans fired back, then galloped away on their horses, leaving the civilian behind. I ran to the man on the ground and asked who he was. 'My name is Juzek. I was taken from my house and charged with sabotage. I was being taken into the forest to be shot.' He stood up and placed his arm around my shoulder for support, though he wasn't hurt badly. I was relieved from duty about an hour later and Juzek was put in charge of the guns and the wireless operating room.

As I sat cleaning my gun one day Maria asked if I was the one who had picked up Juzek. 'Yes, why?', I asked.

'He's very handsome.'

One day I was in the captain's room. Maria walked in and said to the captain: 'I like Juzek very much, but I didn't like the way he acted when I walked into the wireless operating room. I think he was speaking German.'

'Don't be silly', said the captain. 'Juzek was a pre-war staff sergeant in the Polish army.'

A few days later, the Germans attacked the forest. We were always prepared for an attack and quickly took up positions to retaliate. Juzek was in charge of the heavy machine gun. I was lying next to the captain as the Germans approached the forest. The captain told me to have a look at Juzek because he wasn't firing at the Germans. I ran to him shouting: 'Why don't you shoot, Juzek?'

'They're not near enough for me to fire', he answered. But they were getting too near for my liking.

'Shoot or I'll shoot you!', I said.

Trembling, he opened fire, killing a lot of German soldiers. I ran back to the captain: 'Juzek said he wouldn't fire because the Germans weren't close enough. They were almost on top of us! I don't like the way he's acting.' But the captain wouldn't take any notice of what I was saying.

We managed to overpower the Germans, this time.

Not long afterwards Juzek had us clean guns, especially the heavy machine guns. As we were cleaning them the Germans attacked again. The captain, a few of the men and myself tried to surround them, but the Germans opened fire on us. Some of the men managed to pull out, leaving the captain and me behind. We tried to defend ourselves, but it was useless and we were forced to surrender.

Four soldiers escorted us through the city back to their headquarters. We were led into a room where a German lieutenant was waiting for us. The lieutenant rolled a cigarette, looked at Captain Bronowski and asked him, pointing at me: 'Is this your son?'

The captain looked at me: 'Yes.'

The lieutenant walked over to me and said: 'Do you want your father to live?'

'Yes, sir.' He ordered me to tell him who the chief of the underground movement was. 'I don't know, I've never seen him', I said.

He walked over to the captain and asked him: 'Do you want your son to live?'

'Yes, sir.'

'I want you to tell me, captain.'

The captain's answer was the same as mine. 'I don't know as I've never seen him.' The German lost his temper and struck the captain across the face.

'I want the truth!', he screamed. *'Wache! Wache!'*

Four guards came in and the lieutenant told them to make us strip. He took a whip from his desk and gave it to one of the guards, ordering him to give Captain Bronowski five hard lashes on his back. Three of them held his arms out while the other held his head down and whipped him hard.

I noticed a pistol handle, partly covered by a raincoat, sticking out of a holster hanging behind the door. I wanted to reach for it, but wasn't sure if it was loaded. The lieutenant ordered the guards to give me five lashes. They held me down in the same way as they had held the captain. After the second lash I shouted: 'I'll tell you the truth!' The lieutenant ordered the four guards to leave the room.

The lieutenant searched for something in his desk drawer but couldn't find what he was looking for. He turned around to a cupboard fixed to the wall. I reached for the pistol behind the door. Luckily for us it was loaded. 'Stand where you are with your hands up!' He stood trembling because I had given my command in German.

I locked the door from the inside and told him to lie down with his face to the floor. The captain took the German's gun and opened the back window. 'Don't move or I'll shoot you', ordered the captain. As we started out the window I noticed a machine gun in one corner of the room.

'What about that?' The captain took the belt of bullets out of the gun and we made our escape back to the hide-out in the forest, where everyone was waiting for us.

Captain Bronowski sent some of the men to the village with leaflets arranging a meeting inside the old fire station. When we arrived the next morning a large crowd had gathered. The captain made a speech asking people to deliver clothing, food, shoes and anything they could spare to help our cause. While he spoke the Germans had surrounded the station and began shooting at the people inside, killing many of them. We all stood with our hands up when a German lieutenant burst in. The German soldiers pushed us into a corner and the lieutenant looked at our faces.

Juzek had pushed himself to the front of the crowd. He

saluted *'Heil Hitler!'* and the lieutenant said to him: 'You've done a very good job.' We heard shots and saw our men, the ones we had left behind in the forest, surrounding the fire station. The Germans put their hands up, except Juzek, who had run up a ladder. The captain shot him and he was fatally wounded. We disarmed the Germans and took their boots and belts. The soldiers were spared because we knew other Germans would take revenge on the people of the village if they were killed.

Back at our headquarters, I overheard the captain talking to Maria: 'You weren't wrong about Juzek. He was a German spy. I killed him like a dog, the way he deserved to die.'

Another mission was to blow up an ammunition dump in Radom. The mission was a success and we began our three-hour walk back to the forest. I thought that if I were sent on such a dangerous mission again I was sure to be killed. I decided to try to make my way to Aunt Golda's.

I let all the men march past me until I was at the back of the line. I said to the last person: 'Can you hold my gun while I go to the toilet? You keep on marching and I'll catch up with you.' I made my way back to Ostrowiec.

7 · Murder of my Aunt and Uncle

It was early morning on 5 January 1941 when I knocked on my aunt's door. 'Quick, come inside', she said with tears in her eyes. Karol had made it there safely three weeks earlier and he and my aunt and uncle were happy to see me after so long.

'Where is everyone in the family?', my aunt asked.

'They're all dead', I said and she started to cry.

'How do you know?'

'The train they were taken away in took them to Treblinka and the gas chambers.'

'You must try to forget all about it', she said. 'Now you'll have to take care of yourselves.'

I asked why they were able to walk about the streets so freely without being afraid. They told me they had forged identification papers with different names and were living as gentiles. 'Look what has happened to the world', Uncle Revuz declared. 'We are forced to hide and use false names and be afraid to admit we're Jews!'

Four or five days after I had returned to Ostrowiec my aunt heard a commotion outside the house and rushed to the window. 'My God! It's the police!', she screamed. 'They're coming towards the house. Quick, the two of you, get into the attic!' Karol and I ran outside into a small passageway and up a ladder into the attic.

As we reached the top there was banging on the front door and voices shouting 'Open the door!' Uncle Revuz opened the door to four Germans and an officer who demanded to see their documents. While the Germans were asking questions, Karol and I found a small door at the back of the house which led outside. I pushed it open and saw a wooden pole leaning against the side wall of the house.

I slid down the pole to the ground and jumped over the

back garden fence. Hiding behind the fence, I peered through a crack to see where my brother was; I expected him to be behind me. I turned and saw him hanging on the pole with a German policeman pointing his rifle up at him. '*Halt!*', he shouted. I saw my brother's hands slowly slide back down the pole on the other side of the fence. Karol had been caught.

I crouched, waiting for the Germans to go away. I could hear shouting and banging inside the house. I realized I was standing in my pyjamas with the snow almost up to my knees. Eventually I had to tear my pyjama jacket into pieces and wrap it around my feet to keep them from freezing.

'*Raus!*', I heard. 'Get out of here, all of you!' Karol, my aunt and uncle were taken out into the street. I jumped over the fence and tried to get back into the house to get some warm clothes but the door had been locked. A warning label with a skull and cross-bones had been affixed to it. I had to climb back up the pole to the attic door to get back into the house.

I got dressed and ran into the street to see where the Germans were taking them. There they were, my brother, aunt and uncle, being led away by the four policemen. I walked behind at a distance, pretending not to know them. I followed them to the German police station and hid in a doorway. For a long time I watched the door to the police station open and close with SS men coming and going. I couldn't feel my feet; it was still snowing and very cold.

Finally the police station door opened and a policeman, his rifle hanging on his shoulder, came out and held the door open for my brother, followed by my aunt and uncle and another policeman with a rifle on his back. The policeman led them through the small gate at the Ostrowiec prison and came back a little later without them.

I didn't know which way to turn: I had nowhere to go, nowhere to sleep and no one to help me. I couldn't go back to the house in case the Germans returned in the morning to search it. There was only one alternative and that was to go to the Jewish ghetto.

The entrance to the ghetto was guarded by a Jewish policeman. I didn't want to go in at a place where I would have to answer lots of questions, so I walked on the opposite side of the pavement, thinking about the best way to get in without being seen. The ghetto had been fenced off with wardrobe doors and doors from property owned by the Jewish people whom the SS had deported to Treblinka.

At the end of the road I came to the lamppost where I had untied the German horse and fled to the forest. This was the only way I could get back into the ghetto – via that same lamppost. Once inside, no one took any notice of me.

I walked into a building and up to the first floor. There was a large hall full of bunk beds, three-high, and everybody was asleep. I started down the stairs. On my way down, I met a man coming up carrying on his head a round woven basket full of black bread.

I followed him: 'Why are all those men asleep in that room?'

'They do the night shift in the ironworks', he answered.

'Could I work there?'

"You look like a strong boy, so you should have no problem getting work from the Jewish Council. And if you do register with the Council you'll be eligible for food.'

I registered with the Jewish Council and wandered around the ghetto. All I could think about was my brother and aunt and uncle and how to help get them released from prison. By the time I got back to the building where the men were, they were awake. But I was more interested in finding a place to sleep.

I struck up conversation with a man and we talked about many things. When I told him I came from Konin he said: 'There's a man in the corner bunk bed from Konin.'

'What's his name?', I wondered.

'Norman Ancer.'

'I know him, he's a dentist.' I went to the corner to find the man I knew. 'Norman?', I said.

'Srulek? What are you doing here?'

'My brother's in prison. And my aunt and uncle...' I told him the whole story.

'Let's go and see the Jewish police chief', Norman advised. 'We'll see if he can do something to help, because he knows the Gestapo chief and his men.' Norman took me to the Jewish police chief.

When we arrived there were a few Jewish policemen being

46

allocated their duties. 'How are your teeth?', Norman asked the Jewish police chief when we were alone.

'Come here tomorrow and take a look', the chief said. Then he looked at me: 'You are together? What do you want me for?'

'Tell Mr Hoffman what your problem is', Norman said to me.

I went through the whole story again and the Jewish police chief said: 'If you have a lot of gold or gold coins I can do something. I could see if the Gestapo chief would accept anything you might have that is of value for the release of your brother. But your aunt and uncle – that's a different story. You must understand that they have been living as Polish Christians. So it's better we don't talk about them, because if they have denied they are Jewish, I can't talk about their release. They must have produced Polish papers. Perhaps they'll let them go. The only one I could talk about is your brother. But I can't do anything until tomorrow.'

I couldn't wait until the next day. When we left Hoffman, I said to Norman: 'I'm going to my aunt's house and I'm going to search to see if there's anything of value there. At least I can try and save my brother's life.' A lot of people could be bought. Some people would take a bribe, then shoot you anyway.

I made my way through the ghetto fence to the Polish side, without a Star of David armband, and walked through the snow and ice, wondering if the Germans had already searched the house. I found the door of the house wide open. But I still had to take a chance.

Cautiously I walked into the house, but when I looked around I broke down and cried. I noticed through the window a woman coming out of the house opposite my aunt's house. When she looked in my direction something struck me. I rushed to her with tears in my eyes, screaming: 'You tell your husband if I live through this war there will be no place for you or your husband to hide for what you've done, telling the German police that there were Jews living here! I remember both of you, Mrs Szarafinska. You and your husband were always against us Jews. I come from Konin like you do. So don't think I don't know who you are!'

She shouted back at me: 'If you don't go away I'll call the German police again!' I knew I was right. I spat in her face and ran.

By the time I got back to the prison, running through the back streets, it was snowing heavily. I stood in a doorway at a distance and watched the German guard at the prison gates. I watched to see if he would ever leave his guard box but the only time he left was when he got cold – then he would march up and down the length of the prison building.

The guard wore a large duffel coat with fur around the edge of the hood, and a rifle hanging from his shoulder. He blew into his gloves and stamped his feet to keep warm. He marched up and down several times and once walked close to me. I thought he had seen me so I pulled in my stomach to make myself slimmer. At the last moment he marched back towards the sentry box. As he turned, I slipped in behind him and marched with him through the prison gate and into the prison yard.

I was shaking from head to foot, partly with fear, partly from the icy snow. Sneaking over to a prison window, I called quietly 'Karol, Karol'. Karol saw me and was coming to the window when I felt a cold hand grab the back of my neck calling *'Herr Kommandant! Herr Kommandant!'* I didn't know who was holding me so tightly and I tried to free myself. In the struggle my leg caught his leg and he slipped on the ice and fell to the ground. It was the guard. The commandant rushed out from the prison with a Polish-speaking civilian and took me away from the guard.

I was taken into the commandant's office and told to sit. 'Who are you?', he asked. 'What are you doing in the prison yard? Who sent you here?'

'My brother's in the prison', I answered.

'What is his name?'

'Karol Hahn – a young boy', I replied.

'So you are his brother? That means you also are a Jew', he proclaimed.

'Yes.'

He didn't ask any more questions. He wrote everything down and called 'Ludwik! Ludwik!' The Polish civilian warden came in and was told to lock me up in an empty cell. Ludwik walked me through the prison corridors until we came to the last cell; he opened the door, gave me a push, and slammed the heavy door behind me.

I found myself in a large cell, on my own. The cell was freezing. The windows had been smashed and iron bars put up from the outside. I lay down on the wall-to-wall wooden bunk, curled up in one corner to keep warm. Eventually the cell door opened and Ludwik stood in the corridor with an old army churn. He handed me an aluminium pot and filled it with hot soup. He slammed the door again, locking it behind him.

I sat on the bunk drinking my soup, trying to puzzle out how to get through the bars of the window. On closer inspection, it seemed hopeless without tools. I spotted some pieces of broken window pane outside which I could reach if I stretched out my arm. I scraped around the bottom of one of the bars to see if I could free it enough to bend it so that my head would fit through. I dug out the rotten wood from the prison bars and hid all the wood shavings under my cell bunk. I noticed a white shirt, probably belonging to a previous prisoner, lying under the bunk. I screwed the shirt up into a small bundle and pushed it back under the bunk out of sight. Back at the window I put my head in between the iron bars to see if it would go through. I felt I could turn the bar on the window with my hand, and I was excited that I might have a chance of freedom.

I wanted to make my way to the ghetto to see if I could get any help from the Jewish police chief. As I sat on my bunk planning my escape I heard a commotion in the prison corridor. I looked through the spy-hole in the door and saw a lot of men dressed in green uniforms with cases and rucksacks on their backs. They looked like Polish soldiers.

Ludwik, the Polish warden, opened the cell door and the uniformed men pushed themselves into the cell. They were wet and covered with snow but were joking and laughing. The leader of the men went to the window, noticed the missing glass and snow blowing through the prison bars into his face, and ordered the men to stack up the cases in front of the window to stop the snow drifting into the cell.

The men took their places on the bunk, leaving me without any room to sleep. Two of the men came over to me and asked me a lot of questions. I said to them: 'Whatever I tell you, you can't help me because I'm here in this prison to be executed.'

'Holy Mary, Mother of God', they said. 'they aren't going to execute you!'

'You don't know the Gestapo like I do. I have seen human blood flowing through the streets and into the gutters in this town – the blood of innocent men, women and children murdered by the Gestapo.'

One of the men was writing on a scrap of paper so I asked him if I could borrow his pencil. He broke the pencil in half and with a penknife sharpened the half he gave me. I don't even know what made me think of it, but I decided to make myself an armband. I pulled out the old shirt from under the bunk, tore it into narrow strips and drew a Star of David on one of the strips. Jews were required to wear an armband with the Star of David on it and, if you were caught without it, you would be shot on the spot. Neither Karol nor I had one. I made two.

As I was making the second armband I looked out of the window and thought: 'I'm going to die because those men have stopped the escape I was planning. So here I am sitting, condemned, in a cell waiting to be executed.'

'What is today's date?', I asked one of the men.

The man turned to his leader: 'Our friend here wants to know today's date.' He looked in a little book and said: 'Today is 11 January 1941.'

I realized who these men were: a Polish brigade called the Junaks, working under orders from the German authorities. These 12 men had been granted leave for Christmas and the New Year but had been late in reporting back to work. So as their punishment they had been put in prison for two more weeks while they waited to be dispatched to their duties.

I heard a commotion in the prison corridor and ran over to the door to take a look. It was two Gestapo men causing the trouble, but the closer I looked, the closer I was to death: I recognized the two as Officer Wagner and Officer Ostman.

Ludwik was coming towards my cell. Dangling his keys, he

opened the door and shouted: 'Where's the young Jew?' I pushed my way through the men and when I reached the door he looked at me with his one eye and said: 'Your time has come, Jew!'

'I've left my overcoat on the bunk', I told him as I ran back in to get my coat.

'Where you're going you won't need a coat!', he sneered.

I stood with one foot in the cell and one foot in the corridor. 'I tell you, if I survive this war, I will be back here and I'll take out your other eye!'

He slammed the door as the Junaks shouted after him: 'You blind son of a bitch!'

I was led to the German commandant's office and stood in front of Officers Ostman and Wagner. The one-eyed prison warden pushed my brother in through the door. We stood side by side listening to the two Gestapo men making jokes with the commandant. 'You have a very familiar face', one of them said to me. 'I know you from working for our chief – is that right?'

'Yes, sir', I answered as he wrote something in the commandant's book. He asked the commandant for a piece of string. The commandant took a small knife and a ball of twine from his desk drawer and handed it to Ostman. Wagner cut two pieces of string and told us to hold out our hands. He tied our hands together in a way that I could easily undo. He cut another two pieces of string and went out into the corridor.

When he returned Ostman asked him: 'Are you finished?'

'Yes', Wagner replied. Both clicked their heels with a '*Heil Hitler!*' salute.

In the prison corridor we came face to face with my aunt and uncle, who also had their wrists tied. The four of us were led through the narrow prison gate into the street. We walked to the ghetto. We couldn't talk to my aunt and uncle because we knew they had Polish identification papers and were posing as Polish Christians. But my brother and I were known in the ghetto as Jews.

As we walked along the icy road I thought of running away from these two executioners. But I realized that if I ran away I would have to leave my brother and aunt and uncle, so I changed my mind. Also, if I ran I could easily slip on the ice and the Gestapo men would have an easy target to shoot at. I thought: 'If I'm going to die, let me at least die with the last few members of my family.'

A Jewish policeman opened the gate to the ghetto and Ostman told us to stand against a wall while he and Wagner went into the office of the Jewish police chief. Hoffman, the Jewish police chief, returned with the executioners, discussing our situation.

All of a sudden there was a *'Heil Hitler!'* salute. Bending down to get through the small door was Gestapo chief Langer, holding a briefcase under his arm. Ostman and Wagner clicked their heels: *'Heil Hitler!'* Hoffman came to see whom the Gestapo had brought. I said to him in Yiddish: 'Mr Hoffman, the Gestapo chief knows me because your office sent me to work for him a little while ago.'

'Who's this?', Hoffman asked looking at Karol.

'This is my brother.'

'You know those two people standing next to you?', he asked, referring to my aunt and uncle.

With a heavy heart I had to say 'No'. Hoffman returned to the others.

The Gestapo chief kept looking at us and at last he said to me: 'Yes, I remember you. You're a good worker. Where are your armbands?'

'I've got them right here, Herr Langer', I said, reaching into my pocket for the two armbands. He had a smile on his face as Karol and I hurried to put on the armbands.

'Get away. Go on', he said.

Karol and I ran around the corner of an old building to see what they were going to do with my aunt and uncle. We knew we would probably never see them again.

They were led out of the ghetto and put into a car. Later we saw Wagner walk through the gate followed by my aunt and uncle and then Ostman. I knew right away they had been under interrogation because their faces were bruised and they had cuts on their cheeks. Karol and I followed, with tears in our eyes, as they walked towards a wall at the end of the Jewish cemetery.

Wagner and Ostman led but as they neared the wall they

changed positions so that they walked behind my aunt and uncle. Simultaneously they unclipped their pistols from their waists. Still walking and only a few metres from the wall, the two Gestapo men raised their arms, pointed the pistols and fired. My aunt and uncle fell on the snowy ground.

Uncle Revuz tried to get up but was kicked in the head. He tried to cover his head with his arms. My aunt lay motionless. The two Gestapo men stood over their bodies and fired more bullets into their heads just to make sure.

I could only watch the murder of my aunt and uncle with tear-filled eyes. I was sorry I didn't have a gun: I would have done the same to the two Gestapo men. Even if I had had a gun though, I couldn't have shot those two bastards because the rest of the Gestapo would have wreaked havoc in the ghetto. Many innocent people would have been killed in retaliation for the deaths of two Gestapo officers. One of the executioners stood over the still warm bodies of my aunt and uncle while the other pulled the new winter boots off their feet. They called to someone in the ghetto: 'Hey, you, carry these boots!' All I could do was cry to myself. I left my aunt and uncle lying in a pool of blood, trying to figure out how I could get them buried.

Smoke was rising over the wall of the cemetery. Karol and I decided to investigate. At the entrance to the cemetery we found a group of men burning furniture on a plot of land. When I asked the supervisor what was happening he told me to go a bit further into the cemetery and we would see.

There was a huge pile of bodies of executed people, frozen on the ground, waiting to be buried. Among them were women clutching their babies in their arms. We went back to the supervisor: 'We saw all those bodies.'

'That's why we're burning the furniture, to thaw out the ground to dig a mass grave and bury all those frozen bodies. You two boys look strong – we could do with some more help.'

'We will help you but you have to help us too', we told him.

'How can I help you?'

'On the other side of this wall there are two more people who have been executed. I would like them to be buried in the mass grave too.'

'I'll send some men with you to collect the bodies'.

He assembled eight men with stretchers made out of old wooden doors. Aunt Golda was placed on a stretcher first. I tried to take my uncle's arms from his face, but they were already frozen solid. We placed him on a stretcher too and carried them back to the cemetery.

After six days of thawing the ground and digging, we were able to begin burying the frozen dead. Our supervisor went away for a while and returned with a sack on his back. He placed the sack in the snow and took from it a mug and a large bottle of vodka. He asked if anyone wanted a drink and everybody rushed to form a line. As he poured the men were holding his hand so he wouldn't stop pouring the vodka into the mug.

Everybody wanted to get drunk because no one wanted to be sober to bury the bodies, especially the dead women holding their young babies. The burial took another four days and all the men, including ourselves, walked away drunk, tears streaming down our faces.

8 · Clash with Ukrainian Foreman

Karol and I had nowhere to go, no place to sleep, no food to eat. We returned to the Ostrowiec ghetto and managed to survive there for four or five months, until the ghetto was liquidated. After a while we decided the only thing to do was to give ourselves up and go to work in the camp behind the Herman Göring ironworks. At least we'd be able to get some food there. We stayed at the camp for the next 12 months doing various slave-labour jobs.

We were then sent out to work in a train factory in Ostrowiec and were both put in the building department. For a long time we worked on a cement mixer, taking orders from a Ukrainian manager. I was told I must turn out 60 barrels of cement a day, but this was impossible. I was taken off this job and given a wheelbarrow which had to be loaded with bricks and pushed up to the third floor where the builders were laying bricks.

It was summer 1942 and we had been in the train factory some 18 months. We were stripped to the waist as it was a very hot day. The German manager kept shouting at us to keep moving. It was pure and simple slave labour. The manager had a son of 18, who was also one of our foremen. He was like a wild beast. He always stood in the doorway with a stick in his hands. As the men pushed the wheelbarrows, loaded with bricks, through the door he would hit them with the stick on their bare backs, shrieking: 'Get going, you dogs!' We all prayed to God to get rid of him and his father.

When the father came to work he always went into his office first. But one morning he came to where we were working, shouting like a madman, giving orders that the boys were to carry 60 bricks at a time. We did as we were told, but it was impossible to push a wheelbarrow loaded with 60 bricks up to the third floor. Each time we tried, the weight of the bricks pushed us back. Only a few of the boys managed to get to the third floor.

When the manager saw this he walked away. Then one of our own, Jewish foremen came along. I said to him: 'You're supposed to be our foreman and protector. Why don't you speak up for us?'

He gathered us all together and told us what had happened: 'When the manager went home last night, he found that his son had been called up for the German army and is to be sent to the Russian front. This is his way of getting his revenge.' He told us to carry 30 bricks at a time and he would go straight to the manager's office to talk it over with him. Some 20 minutes later our foreman and the manager came out of the office. Without saying a word they walked away.

I said to one of the lads: 'Even this load is too much to push up to the third floor. Make out you can't do it.' I turned my wheelbarrow over with all the bricks in it and they fell from the third floor.

One of the Ukrainian foremen saw me drop the bricks and hit me across the back with a stick. I felt the pain shoot through my body. I didn't care what would happen – I picked up a brick and threw it right in his face. He fell to the ground and I could see his face was covered in blood.

I was scared and looked at my brother. 'What did you do that for?', shouted Karol, frightened for the pair of us.

'Never mind what I did it for! Let's get out of here!' We ran around the factory looking for a place to get over the high walls, but it was impossible. We ran back to the place where we had been working. I saw a crowd of Ukrainian guards putting the foreman on a stretcher. We stood frozen with fear, sweat pouring down our faces. Just then a train loaded with machinery was pulling out of the factory.

'Quick, jump on to one of the trucks!', I yelled to Karol. We moved without saying a word to each other, and we sat waiting, hiding among the machinery.

The train pulled out of the factory, but backed on to another line. Before long I heard a whistle and the train started to move slowly. I looked around. When the train passed the factory gates, I said to Karol: 'Quick, let's jump off before the train goes any faster.' We jumped off safely into deep grass.

'What are we going to do now?', Karol asked.

Karol and I had to wait for a train to sneak back inside the factory, as we had escaped before. A train loaded with scrap metal came along and when it stopped, waiting for the guards to open the gates, we jumped on top of the trucks and hid until the train was inside the factory.

A group of men and women were coming to work from the labour camp near the Ostrowiec ghetto. Some of the men were surprised to see Karol and me after all this time, thinking we were dead. I asked one of them what had happened after I threw the brick in the foreman's face. He told me the whole camp had been searched, but it was quiet now and I shouldn't have any trouble. We didn't want to take any chances, so we slept in the factory where we wouldn't be seen. Factory workers who lived outside the camp brought us food.

A few weeks later, we were in the large dining room of the labour camp. Two Ukrainian guards walked in; one stood at the door while the other walked around the dining room shouting at everyone to keep quiet. We didn't know who he was looking for until he came over to me and ordered me to go with him.

As I got to the door, the guard pushed me with his rifle and told me to move faster. They escorted me to the factory guard room where I was put in a cell and locked up until the following morning. When the night shift was being marched back to the camp, I was put in front of the group, escorted by two Jewish policemen, and marched to the camp. All the workers were counted out – except me. They were sent back to their sleeping quarters; I was taken to a room without windows and locked up again.

I sat there for a few hours wondering what would happen to me when I heard shouting: '*Achtung!*' I knew the German camp commandant had arrived. A few minutes later the door to my room opened. Standing there was one of our camp police. 'Come out, you're going to the *Verwaltungsführer.*'

As I walked from the building all the people in the labour camp were standing outside their barracks. I had to go to the German camp commandant. The Jewish camp chief, Abram

Zaifman, was there with him waiting for me. As I walked in, I saw the commandant hand Zaifman a cigar. The two were good friends. I stood in the corner while they they were having a good laugh. I felt happier because they were laughing and appeared to be in a good mood.

'Welcome home!', Zaifman shouted and threw an ash-tray at me, shattering it into pieces. 'You're one of the tough boys, aren't you? You want to show the others you're a hero, that nothing can happen to you!' He kept on shouting but I didn't say a word.

The commandant said to Zaifman: 'Don't lose your temper. We can settle this quietly.' Then he turned to me: 'I'm going to have you shot like a dog with all the other people watching.'

I knew he meant it. He sat down and told me to turn my face to the wall. A few minutes later I heard them laughing again. Then Zaifman told me to turn round. He said: 'The commandant's going to let you off for one reason – the man whose face you threw the brick at weighs about 14 stone and if a young boy like you has the pluck to do a thing like that to such a big man, we're going to let you off.'

I thanked Zaifman in German and opened the door ready to go. Zaifman told me to wait as he wrote something on a piece of paper and handed it to me. He gave me permission to go to the kitchen for food. He said that from then on I should behave myself and, if I did anything wrong again, I would be shot.

I went straight to the camp kitchen where all the people I knew were waiting for me, happy to see me alive.

My mind still wouldn't let me rest and I started thinking how I could get away from them and be free again. But they hadn't finished with me yet. A few hours later Karol and I were called into the chief's office. Zaifman sat, staring hard at us. 'Tell me what's on your mind', I said, but he didn't answer. 'What order have you given that my brother and I should not be let out of the camp to work in the factory?'

He smiled: 'That's exactly what I wanted to say. I can't let you work out of the camp together, only one at a time, because you'll disappear again. You're not responsible for me, but I am responsible for you.'

'I'm unlucky I can't get out. If I could, I'd go for good. It's alright for you, sitting here behind a desk giving orders while we're doing the slave work in the factory and being treated worse than dogs.'

'This is a labour camp and everybody must work', he answered coldly. 'Now you're finished with that job in the factory, I'm going to give you a job here in the camp.' I asked him what it was and he screamed: 'Never mind what it is! Whatever job is given to you, you will do it! Your job will be in the baths looking after the boilers with two other men. Your brother will have a job in the kitchen. You'll start work tomorrow. Now go.'

One evening, three men and I were sent out to the factory in a truck, under the watch of two guards, to collect coal for the camp baths. When we returned I noticed many people were by the camp gates. I jumped off the truck and asked what was going on. One of the guards had been strangled to death. Some of the other guards had been tied up and locked in a dark room, and all the ammunition had been taken. It was rumoured to have been the underground movement. I walked away thinking what a good chance I'd missed: I could have escaped with them.

After that incident the guards turned a bit softer and came inside the camp in an attempt to be friendly with the inmates. When I saw them walking about the camp, I just couldn't stand them. They were really coming into the camp not to make friends, but to spy. They wanted to see if any of us were wearing jewellery or had any other valuables.

A few days later the gates were locked from the outside and the guards were doubled. For two days no one was allowed to leave the camp and in the morning of the second day all of us were gathered in the camp square. Three cars arrived; the passengers were the German camp chief and two Gestapo men. One of the camp police standing inside the gate shouted '*Achtung!*'

We all had to stand to attention immediately, and it made no difference where we were standing, until the visitors had walked into the Jewish chief's office. They were there over an hour before we saw them come out and walk to the middle of the camp. Our chief was with them. Then about 50 guards marched into the camp with five long tables. They carried the tables over to the SS men and on the tables they put empty cases. The guards went from barrack to barrack ordering people to the central area of the camp again. We were surrounded by guards to make sure no one went back into the barracks.

One of the Gestapo men stood on a table and shouted: 'We've put these tables here for a reason. You probably don't know why, so I'm going to tell you. Everybody is going to pass between the tables and anybody who has on them any gold, diamonds, dollars or English pounds must put them into the cases on the tables. What's more, everybody will be searched and if they hide anything and refuse to give it up they will be shot here and now in front of everyone. Now, everybody form a queue!'

The Germans knew where to go because a number of the people in the camp were very rich. Some of them were giving jewellery away to people who had none, telling them to hide it, and 100-dollar notes, but I wouldn't take them. A woman offered me a diamond and said: 'Go on, have it. Do whatever you like with it. I would sooner give it to you than them.' 'Alright', I said, 'I'll take it. But once I pass the table, and they don't find it on me, don't come back for it later. I'm not going to risk my life for you.' I put the diamond in my mouth, tore off a piece of my old shirt and held it over my cheek as though I had toothache. When my turn came, my pockets were searched and I was passed. The cases were almost filled with jewellery.

It was dark before the search was complete. The guards left the camp and we were allowed back into the barracks. Orders were given for the night shift to prepare for work. Everything went back to normal for a while.

9 · Deportation to Auschwitz

One morning in mid-summer 1942, as I passed by the chief's office, I saw people reading a notice on the wall. It said we were to pack all our belongings and get ready because the entire camp was going to be evacuated. A rumour went around that we were supposed to be going by train to Germany to work in a munitions factory, but it was a lie.

My brother came to the baths where I worked and called me out: 'I don't like the sound of that notice the chief put on the wall. I'm sure it's all lies.'

'We'll probably have a chance to get away from the train', I reassured him.

'Yes, but it depends how many guards there are.'

I told him I had a different idea: 'If we're inside the train, we'll try to get out as it's moving.' I thought I should make a parcel with some tools in case we needed them – perhaps a small saw, a hammer and a pair of pliers. I had a few tools I had collected from the factory.

'I hope you're right. I hope we can get off the train, because wherever we go we'll have to slave.' He didn't know the half of it.

I told Karol to go to the barracks and bring me the two blankets we slept under. I told him the best way to make the parcel was to put the tools in one blanket, cover it with the other and sew the edges together. Then we would be ready to go; I would just throw the bundle over my shoulder. It wouldn't be noticeable as we had no other parcels. We did everything just as I said.

Three days later, the second shift returned from the factory at ten o'clock in the evening and the night shift was due to go out. As they started out the gate they were stopped by one of the guards. 'I've just had a phone call', he said. 'I'm not allowed to let anyone out of the camp until further notice.'

The next morning the guards told us to meet in the middle of the camp in half an hour. The guards were Ukrainians; they were as 'kind' to us as the Germans. When we were gathered together the German commandant called for Zaifman, the Jewish camp chief. But Zaifman was gone. The rumour was that he, his wife and their little boy had vanished fom the camp during the night.

We marched to the ironworks factory where there was a long train with covered cattle trucks waiting for us. I feared the worst. The guards formed us into groups of 50 and began loading the train. Karol and I fell into the group with the Jewish camp police. The door of the truck was closed behind us.

I could hear footsteps from the guards positioned above us on the roof. The train stood still for only a short while, the whistle blew and the journey began. Everyone in our truck fell asleep except my brother and me. We opened the blanket and took out the tools.

'There's only one way out of here', I said. 'It's not a fast train and if everything goes the way I figure, we can get out very quickly.'

'How?', Karol asked.

'There's only one way – we have to cut through the floor as we are sitting here.'

'Have you gone mad?', Karol whispered. 'How can we do a thing like that with all these Jewish policemen around us?'

Looking at the faces of the sleeping Jewish policemen, I knew we had to try: 'Listen, Karol, it's our last chance to get away!'

'What good will it do? We should stay and see what's going to happen next.' But I didn't take any notice of my brother.

In the morning no one said a word, waiting for something to happen. 'How many of you would like to get out of here?', I asked.

'We all want to get out of here', someone answered. 'But how?' I told them it would be easy if they all agreed. I took the saw and started to saw in one corner of the truck. I wanted to cut a small square out of the floor so we could let ourselves down between the lines as the train moved.

*

After a journey of three days the train stopped, everything went quiet and I hid the saw. It must have been a few hours before I heard the guards jump from the top of the train. Bells rang out and the doors on both sides of the truck were opened. I saw people walking about in striped uniforms behind a barbed-wire fence. I knew we had come to a large concentration camp but we didn't know which one until the SS men took over the transport.

The Ukrainians who had been guarding the train were disarmed and marched away. There were whistles and shouts from the SS; everyone was to get off the train and leave all their personal belongings behind. As we jumped off the train some of the people tried to bring along food or anything else they had taken with them. The SS men shouted at them: 'Leave everything behind! Where you're going you won't need anything! *Das ist Auschwitz Konzentrations Lager und nicht ein Spielplatz!* (This is Auschwitz concentration camp, not a playground!)' They shouted at us to form lines of three.

'Everything in order?', shouted one of the SS men.

'Yes, sir. Forward march! One, two, three, four, left, left...'

We marched about a quarter of a mile and passed through a gate adorned with an eagle and a swastika. '*Arbeit macht frei*' framed the top of the gate. 'Work will make you free' would soon become a haunting slogan for prisoners lucky enough to escape the gas chambers.

We were marched to a large, isolated bathhouse and told to form a single line and walk through a set of double doors. I saw people walking in through the front door but no one seemed to be coming out. Panic started to spread. Everyone thought this was the gas chambers.

I got nearer and nearer until finally I was inside; Karol was right behind me. One of the SS guards shouted: 'Take off your clothes and throw them on top of the others, but keep your shoes with you.' We undressed and held our shoes in our hands. That is all I had on me, the shoes and the diamond I had put in my mouth.

The next stop was the barbers, who were also prisoners. They shaved our hair off right down to the scalp. From there we had to walk through another door, but before we went in we had to dip our shoes into a hole in the floor filled with disinfectant. As we bent down two SS men standing either side of the door with whips hit everybody across the back, our first lesson in camp discipline.

We were rushed into a big tiled bath for a shower. Then we were herded through a different door for clothes. As we walked in, naked, SS women guards were standing there as we took the clothes that were piled up on the floor.

We each received a black shirt with fine white stripes, a jacket and trousers with white and blue stripes and a round hat, similar to a French beret, to match. We had to go outside to dress. We were broken-hearted, but we had to laugh at the way everybody was dressed in striped suits like pyjamas. Some of the men had suits with the jacket sleeves reaching to the elbow, and the trouser legs to the knees. I had a jacket and trousers which a 20-stone man could have fitted into. We made fun of each other and exchanged suits until everybody had the best fit possible.

We had to wait a few hours until all the other prisoners went through the same ordeal. I asked two prisoners who walked by what the two big buildings with the square chimneys were. 'We will all, most probably, come out as smoke through them', was all they said. But that was enough.

'Thanks for those happy thoughts!', I said. The two prisoners walked away laughing to themselves. They had been in Auschwitz for a long time and were used to it. They walked about as if it were a convalescent home and didn't stop to worry about what might happen tomorrow.

Whistles and shouts from the SS guards jarred me back from my thoughts: we had to form ourselves into threes again. Then the command was given for us to march. We marched until it was dark and we were very tired.

Auschwitz was a camp of enormous proportions. All the various nationalities were kept apart from each another. We were taken to our barracks, which we shared with Hungarians whom we, as Poles, were allowed to mix with. We stopped outside and they counted us in – 500 to a barracks.

As we passed through the door the guards hit people whenever they could get at them. There was one small window at the back of the barracks – no beds or blankets, just bare floors, like a stable for horses. We had to make ourselves as comfortable as we could on the hard damp floorboards.

We lay there until four in the morning without anything to eat or drink. Then a prisoner came in wearing the same clothes as us and screamed in German: '*Raus! Raus!* Outside for roll call!' He was not an ordinary prisoner, but a deserter from the German army. There were a lot of them there; they were given the rank of *Kapo* (often an ex-prisoner, a *Kapo* was a foreman appointed by the camp SS to oversee the prisoners). There was a *Kapo*, or foreman, some of whom were Jewish, for every barracks.

We stood for an hour before the SS men arrived to take our numbers. The Kapo ordered us to stand to attention and take our hats off, just like in the German army.

When the SS men arrived, we all stood in threes facing them. The *Kapo* shouted in German: 'Attention! Hats off!' Everything had to be done in exact time. Then the *Kapo* gave his report to the SS on how many men were standing. One of the SS men counted the prisoners himself, looking right into our faces. If he didn't happen to like the look of someone's face as he counted, he would slap it for them. The *Kapo* gave a shout for us to turn right and begin marching.

We marched for about a mile until we came to a large barracks. We formed a single line and walked into the barracks, one after another, between tables. There were other prisoners there already, sitting at small tables with SS men standing next to them. The *Kapo* shouted: 'Everybody pull up your left sleeve and get ready to be numbered.'

The prisoners passed in front of the tables until it was my turn; Karol was right behind me. I put my left arm out and didn't look. It felt as if the pain from the needles was going through my entire body. The number B4258 was printed on my arm. Karol's number was one higher. At first I didn't realize what the number was. It looked like it was written in ink and I tried to rub it off. I realized at that moment that I had become prisoner B4258.

When everyone had been numbered we were taken back to the barracks by the *Kapo*. Inside he told us all to listen carefully: 'We have an inspection here twice a day. When you hear the whistle you will come outside the barracks and form into lines of three. Food is twice a day. One pint of soup and, in the evenings, a pint of black tea and a two-ounce slice of black bread. Sometimes a teaspoonful of jam or margarine. In the mornings, half an hour before roll call you'll have a pint of black tea. Now, everybody line up in single file and give me your name as you pass my table.'

At the mention of names I turned to Karol: 'Give yourself a different surname.'

'What for?'

'If we give the same name they'll probably separate us.' When we got to the table we gave our names as Każek Jankowski, the surname of a friend of mine in Konin, and Karol Ham. We went outside the barracks and waited until everybody had filed through. No questions were asked. A camp *Kapo* came along with another prisoner and asked if we were from blocks 51 and 52: 'I have an order that the prisoners from these two blocks must go to work.' He went inside the barracks and came out a few minutes later with our *Kapo*.

The *Kapo* shouted: 'Form into threes! Turn right, march!' We marched for about two miles until we came to a women's camp. Some of the women came over to talk to us, telling us their names in case we should meet their husbands or sons back at the camp. They begged us to pass on messages that they were still alive and that we had seen them. I too had been asking around for people I knew, giving my name in case anyone was looking for me. Even after having seen my mother board the train for Treblinka I still thought that maybe a miracle would happen. There wasn't time, however, on this occasion for such chatter and we were ordered to move on by the uniformed SS women.

We were taken to a field with thousands of tons of heavy square stones. The foreman ordered each of us to pick up two stones, which weighed about 12 pounds each. But I wasn't listening to what the *Kapo* said. I wasn't in the least bit interested, because when I saw the bare fields and no guards in sight I thought about escaping with my brother. The other prisoners were picking up the stones as they had been told.

'Hey, you two!', I heard behind me. I turned around and saw the *Kapo* coming towards us. 'What are you thinking? How to get out of here? You see fields and no guards so you think it's easy, that there is nobody here? But just you try and run and then you will see how many guards there are with Alsatian dogs guarding Auschwitz.'

We picked up one stone each, but the *Kapo* told us to pick up another one. All the other men had stones in their hands and were ready to march away. We carried the stones until some of the men fainted from exhaustion. We had to wait until they came around and were able to pick themselves up before we could march on. We took a different route back to the camp.

We walked through gate after gate until we were near a large brick building with high square chimneys. It looked like a factory from the outside. The building was surrounded by a barbed-wire fence with blankets hanging over it. I could see smoke and smell a horrible stench which made me feel sick. When I looked between the blankets, inside the wire perimeter I could see long boards lying on the ground and prisoners pushing wheelbarrows with smoking ashes in them along the boards. I heard these were the gas chambers.

The chimneys were not there just to burn rubbish; they were there to liquidate the people that were of no use to them. The ashes were easy to dispose of and they were scattered anywhere – lakes, forests, fields – so there would be no evidence. The only traces of bodies were in the graves. But how many people were scattered in the lakes and forest?

We walked on past the chimneys until we came to a narrow gate. The *Kapo* told us to walk in single file through the gate and said that none of us was to touch the wires because, if we did, we would be burnt to death. We were walking through the gate very carefully when the man in front of me let the stone he was carrying fall to the ground and he threw himself on to the wires. In a split second he had turned as black as coal. Another man threw his bricks down and ran over to try and pull him away, but he was also unlucky. When he put his hands on the other man he stuck to him like glue. He too was dead.

The *Kapo* shouted: 'Get moving!' He stopped at the place where the two dead men were hanging on the wires until we had all passed the gate. The *Kapo* ran in front of the work detail to show us where to put the stones. We stood in threes like soldiers until the *Kapo* gave the command to march, through a different gate, back to our barracks.

At the barracks we had to wait outside for roll call. We stood there only about ten minutes before we heard the bells ringing and shouts for everybody to get ready for the inspection; our group was ready. Shouts of '*Achtung!*' meant the SS had arrived. We waited an hour and a half until they reached our group.

'*Achtung!* Hats off!', shouted the *Kapo*. He reported to the SS that 498 prisoners were ready for roll call.

'There should be 500', growled the SS officer.

'One of the prisoners didn't want to live any longer so he threw himself on to the live wires. Another one tried to pull him off. He died in the attempt.'

The SS officer shouted so that we could all hear: 'It's a pity all of them here don't do that: it would save us work in the gas chambers.' He walked over to the prisoners, wrote down how many there were, then walked away to the next block.

We stood in the same spot until we heard the camp bells ring again, indicating the end of roll call. The *Kapo* picked out eight men and I was among them. The rest of the men were released to the barracks and the eight of us were to go with him to the kitchens.

Outside the kitchens we joined a line of hungry prisoners moving slowly along until we were inside. One of the men joked: 'Smells lovely in here, doesn't it? I could do with roast duck, baked potatoes and peas.'

'Wait a minute', I said, 'I'll tell one of the waiters to reserve a special table for you.'

Another man was getting annoyed: 'Why don't you stop it, you're making my mouth water.'

Then a man leaning against the wall with his eyes closed and his head in the air sniffing in the steam from the boiling soup said: 'Keep on talking, boys, keep on talking. With you talking and me sniffing the steam, it makes me feel as if I'm really eating roast duck and potatoes!'

Our day-dreaming was interrupted by the *Kapo* who told us to take the alloted soup and bread for our barracks. We walked back to the barracks and waited outside until the *Kapo* arrived. We were told to leave the soup churns outside and put the bread on a table in his room. There he cut the bread into the smallest possible pieces. Each loaf weighed about eight pounds, which he cut into pieces of one or two ounces, one piece for each prisoner. He walked outside and stood guarding the churns with a ladle in his hand. The ladle held exactly one pint of soup. As each prisoner's turn came, he held out his bowl and the *Kapo* poured in one ladleful of soup. Not everyone had a bowl and those who didn't had to wait until somebody else finished eating to use their bowl. When everybody had been fed the *Kapo* shouted: 'Form into threes!

Another *Kapo* announced to our foreman: 'I'm taking them to work.' Our *Kapo* turned around to us eight men who had brought the churns from the kitchen and told us to return them and be back in five minutes. We rushed over to the empty churns and started back to the kitchen. Some of the prisoners ran after us, putting their hands into the empty churns, wiping every last drop and licking their hands. Many of them had been at Auschwitz for about two years and looked like skeletons. They were lucky no *Kapos* were about, for if they had seen them they would have beaten them severely with sticks.

We ran back to the barracks, where the prisoners were ready to march away. We had to go back to carry more stones. We did this day after day and I saw that some of the older prisoners were getting weaker and weaker.

One day I noticed some 60 or 70 Italian Jews sitting on a green bank next to the deadly perimeter wires. They obviously didn't have any idea where they were since one of them was conducting the group as they sang beautiful operatic arias. They thought they were in a labour camp and would be out in a few months. I watched, thinking how naïve they were. I'd never seen anyone sitting in a death camp singing arias as they breathed in the stench of burning flesh floating from the chimneys! If they had had only a little understanding, they could have realized what was happening.

They had orchestras in some camps, making out that we were living the good life, but this was only for the blind. It was to keep us from realizing what would happen if they didn't want you. You could be sent to the gas chambers or executed in a forest somewhere at any time – but the orchestra played on. They wanted it all to go on quietly.

Wherever I went I carried the diamond in my mouth, but I could see it was no use to me. Whenever I saw a prisoner with two slices of black bread I would ask him to sell me one of the slices. He would ask what I had to exchange – soup or margarine perhaps. I would take the diamond out of my mouth and show it to him. I offered my diamond to one man, saying: 'I have no soup or margarine, I only have this diamond. Go on, take it, it's worth a lot of money. You'll probably get more for it than I can because you've been here longer and you know better where to sell it.'

He laughed at me: 'You eat the diamond and I'll eat the slice of bread and we'll see who feels better, you or me.' I understood him perfectly.

10 · Escape with Help of an SS Man

It was the autumn of 1942. Karol and I watched an old grey-haired SS man in the guard room, which stood high above the ground on posts, behind our barracks. Each time I saw him he was eating. Once he caught us watching. 'Hey you, catch!', he yelled, throwing something out of the window. Before I could catch anything prisoners behind me tried to get to it first. But no one caught anything: it was only a slice of white bread which had broken up into many pieces.

The guard shouted to me again 'Catch!' and the prisoners fought over another piece of bread. The old SS man walked down from his post with a third slice of bread in his hand and, when the other prisoners saw him coming, they crowded by the barbed-wire fence. This time he didn't throw the bread but pointed to me and said: 'If any of you come closer to the barbed wire except him, I will shoot.' The other prisoners walked away.

'Here you are. Catch the bread!', he said and he threw it over the wire. I caught it and started to walk away when he called after me: 'Stay here and eat it, because if you walk away you will have nothing.'

'But my brother is here, I want to share it with him.'

He told me to eat it and said that when he came on guard duty the next morning he would bring some bread for my brother too. I stood by the wire and ate the precious bread. 'Where do you come from?', he asked.

'From a town called Konin.'

'What is your name?'

'Hahn', I replied.

He gave a restrained shout: 'My God, you have the same name as me!'

'Yes', I said, 'we may have the same name, but the only difference is that you are a German and I am a Jew.'

He looked at me with tears in his eyes: 'To me it makes no difference if you are a Jew, because I am not one of these German Nazis. I was brought up in the reign of Wilhelm, whom you would not remember. If I had my way I would free all you prisoners. What's more, my wife had relatives who were Jews.'

'Even with what you've told me I still don't believe your name is the same as mine.'

He showed me his army book which had his identification photo inside: 'Now do you believe me?'

I looked at the book and to my surprise we did have the same name. 'Yes', I said, uninterested in this new-found comradeship. 'So what's the good of it? Why should I be happy that you have my name? You're free and I'm a prisoner.'

'I can help you get out of here.'

'I suppose you want to take me out behind the wire and shoot me so you can get a medal from your chief!'

'I wouldn't do a thing like that to a young boy like you. I have five sons a bit older than you and how do I know they're not prisoners somewhere, like you are here? They're all in the army on the front line and I haven't heard anything from them.'

'If you're such a good man', I said, 'try and get me and my brother out of here. If you do that I will give you something to make it worth your while.'

'What is it?' I took the diamond out of my pocket and threw it to him. 'Even if you didn't give me a diamond I would still try and get you out of here', he said and threw the diamond back to me.

I threw the diamond back again: 'Keep it, it's no use to me. Here comes another SS man.'

'He's coming to relieve me from duty', said the old guard. 'I will see you tomorrow. When you come back I will tell you what we're going to do.'

Back in the barracks, after the evening inspection, Karol and I were lying on our hard wooden beds when he asked me: 'What was your conversation with the SS man all about?'

'I will tell you tomorrow in case somebody hears us', I whispered. 'As much as I don't trust the SS man, that's how much I don't trust some of the prisoners.'

At morning roll call the *Kapo* announced: 'When roll call is

72

over nobody move because all of you are going to do different work.' So we all stood waiting until two high-ranking SS officers arrived outside our barracks.

'Everybody strip down to the waist', the *Kapo* shouted. He brought two chairs for the Gestapo and they lit cigars. 'Form a single line!' We had to parade in front of the SS officers. They looked closely at the build of our bodies and one of the SS men pointed as the prisoners passed in front of him, giving instructions in German: 'To the left. To the right.'

The prisoners who went to the right were told to stay where they were; the ones on the left were to walk away. As we walked away, being on the left side, I said to Karol: 'I don't understand what they've just done. They've picked out the prisoners who weren't too strong. I wonder what they're going to do with them.'

'What can they do with them?', Karol replied. 'Either they're taking them to work or they're going to the crematorium.'

'We'll soon find out.'

The prisoners who had been picked out were standing in their places and a table had been put in front of them. Then we heard one of the SS officers tell the prisoners to give the numbers tattooed on their arms to the *Kapo* at the table. I went close to the table where the papers were to see if I could sneak a look at them. 'Buna-Monowitz Rubber Plant' was written on the top of the paper where the numbers were being noted. 'They're going to work in a rubber factory', I told Karol.

'I wish they'd picked us with the others.'

'You're wrong. We're better off here.'

'Why?'

I explained: 'Yesterday you asked me about the conversation I had with that old SS man standing by the wires.'

'Yes?'

'If all goes well, we may be out of here in a couple of days and be free again.'

'You're mad!', Karol hissed. 'Have you gone off your head?'

'Why?'

'How can I believe you – that we can get out of here? There are 33,000-volt electrical wires all around us! Especially after what happened to those other two prisoners who were electrocuted!'

'You do talk silly, Karol. I don't mean that way at all. Wait until I talk to the old man again.'

'What's it got to do with him?'

'He is the one who wanted to help us get out of here.'

'Now I can see you really are mad! Surely you would not trust our lives to that old SS man!'

'I think you're the one who's mad, not me. What have we got to lose? We've lost everything we had, so we may as well take a chance. I would sooner try to get out with the help of this SS man than be put in the gas chamber and burnt like a piece of steak.'

Karol was frightened but he knew I was right. 'If you want it that way, we'll try.'

'I'm watching out for the old man now. He'll be on duty soon and, what's more, I gave him the diamond.'

'Did he take it?'

'He didn't want to take it. He said he would get us out of here without it. But I made him take it.'

'I hope you know what you're doing.'

I walked behind the barracks, near the wire, and sat down between two other prisoners, waiting for the SS man to come on duty. A few moments later he came along to relieve the other guard. I waited until it was all clear then walked over to the wire so the guard could see me. 'I've got everything fixed', he said softly so that only I could hear. I was getting anxious and wanted to know all the details of the guard's plan to help us escape from Auschwitz.

'Don't worry', he said. 'Everything will be alright. I'll take you and your brother through all the camps until we get to the last one. This will lead you to a cattle train standing next to the guard room and the kitchen, but I'm afraid I can't get you through the guard room. You won't be able to get through the wires because the guard room barracks are between the wires. If you want to go outside you'll have to walk through the guard room first.'

'How can we get through the wires?', I asked.

'When I go off duty I'll come alongside the gate and call you out. I'll give you two brooms and you'll pretend you're sweeping the ground between the wires. Then you can lift the wires with the handles of the brooms and move out between them. But don't touch the wires or you'll be killed.'

It sounded like a good plan. 'You just come for us and don't let us down and I'll take care of the wires.' I wasn't going to let a little thing like 33,000 volts of electricity stop us now.

'I have one more thing to tell you before I take you out', the old guard added. 'I won't be able to tell you anything else because you'll have to walk in front of me. When you get out and come to the cattle train, don't get inside the train. Get underneath one of the wagons and hold on to anything you can until the train gets out of the Auschwitz district. When the train leaves here it goes under a bridge. On top of the bridge are two SS officers looking into every one of the cattle trucks as the train passes under the bridge.'

'Thank you for that information. This is probably the last time we'll talk to each other.' I was grateful to be able to trust Herr Hahn.

'Good luck', he said sincerely.

'Thank you. I hope we'll be lucky.' I walked outside the barracks and called Karol to one side: 'I've fixed everything.'

'When do we start?'

'We'll have to wait near the gate until we see the old SS man come along.'

We waited impatiently next to a barracks with easy access to the gate. I saw our accomplice coming towards us. Karol and I walked nearer the gate. I saw another guard talking to him and the old SS man pushed the gate open and shouted: 'Hey, you two. Come with me!'

We marched from one camp to another until we stopped outside the kitchen and guard room. The SS man walked into the kitchen and returned with two brooms. A cook came out of the kitchen and lit a cigarette. The old SS man continued with the plan. 'Sweep this area clean!', he shouted.

The cook intervened: 'Better let them clear all these old boxes and barrels to one side.' The guard agreed and the cook showed us how he wanted the boxes stacked, but he told us in a way that was to our advantage. As we cleared broken wood and old butter barrels I noticed a window next to the wire. I stacked the wooden boxes high enough to block the window so the guards inside the barracks couldn't see out.

I heard a train whistle. 'Right, we're getting out', I whispered.

'I'll lift the wires and you get out', Karol said anxiously.

'I have a better idea. You lift the wires and I'll take one of the barrels and put it in between the wires and you drop the wires back on to the barrel. We'll crawl through the barrel. Is that easy enough?'

'It couldn't be easier.' He carefully lifted the wires with the broom and I pushed one of the barrels between the 33,000 volts of electricity. We crawled through. We pulled the barrel from the wires, stacked it in a corner then reached for our brooms and started sweeping again, walking until we came close to the train.

We threw away the brooms and ran to a carriage close to the engine reserved for the SS guards. I pushed myself underneath the train between the springs of the carriage. Karol did the same. As I lay there I heard German voices. It was the engine drivers standing next to the carriage testing and oiling the wheels.

I held on for my life, sweating, my heart banging hard, not from fear, but excitement, waiting for the moment the train would pull away from the death camp. As the train started up, we couldn't hear ourselves talk over the puffing of the steam engine. Karol shouted to me: 'I hope and pray the train starts moving soon or we'll get caught and burn in the oven.'

I pushed him: 'Keep quiet for God's sake, you're making me nervous.' The train pulled away. With every puff the engine gave I felt happier. We lay there until the train stopped once and then again. The second time I looked out from underneath I saw a station full of people on one side of the tracks and open fields on the other. 'Let's get off now – we can't take the chance of going any further. We don't know where this train may go next.' We crawled out from under the train just as it started to move again.

We ran through a grassy field and jumped into a ditch. We waited there until dark when all the people had left the station. We walked until we saw a house near a small village, but as we approached the house we heard a dog barking so we ran off for fear of being discovered. Through the fields at the back of the village we came to a farm. We walked into the farmyard. I heard a door open and a man emerged from a stable with a burning paraffin lamp. He blew out the lamp as he walked across the farmyard into his house. While Karol stood watch, I walked over to the stable and slowly opened the door. Inside two glassy eyes stared at me. I ran back to Karol: 'It's a big stable full of straw and on the other side is a long cage with chickens and there's a big cow lying down.'

'Can we stop here for the night? I'm really tired'.

I agreed. We walked slowly to the stable, making sure we were neither seen nor heard.

'I can smell boiled potatoes', Karol announced with delight.

'I think you're right. You get on top of that straw and I'll have a look around.'

It was very dark in the stable when the doors were shut and I felt my way around like a blind man. I tripped and fell into a small water tank and, as I tried to lift myself out, I felt my hand getting warmer as I discovered the cooked potatoes. I took the corner of my jacket, filled it up with the potatoes and found my way back to Karol.

The straw was high and I couldn't get on top easily. 'Give me a hand and pull me up. I've got supper', I whispered.

'What have you got? Anything good to eat?'

'Yes, we're going to have a party', I said, settling into the prickly straw. 'I've got warm potatoes in their skins.'

'Great!' Karol grabbed the potatoes. 'This is delicious. I couldn't wish for anything better – I'm starving. Can we stop here for a few days?'

'We'll see how we feel in the morning. We must get a long way from here, to a place where there are no Germans. We have no chance hiding around here.'

After we had eaten the potatoes we buried ourselves deep in the straw and went off to sleep.

'Quick! It's roll call!', I shouted, pushing Karol as I woke up sharply from a nightmare.

He jumped up, looked at me and smiled. 'You're crazy, you're dreaming. Don't you remember – we escaped?'

'You're right. I must have been dreaming.'

'I had a fright myself, but not about being in the camp. I thought you were off your head.'

'I probably am mad and don't know it', I smiled. 'How do you feel after last night's supper?'

'As fit as a fiddle', Karol said, looking down for more potatoes. Can you see what I can see? I can see eggs. I'm going to get them and we can drink them out of the shells.'

Just then the door opened and a man with a basket hanging on his arm walked in, limping. He went to the chicken cage, taking the eggs out and putting them into his basket, all the while whistling *Deutschland über Alles*. Then he walked over to the cow and took the rope from around her neck, saying in German 'Get out.' The cow walked out and he followed, leaving the door open.

Karol turned to me: 'I'm very sorry, sir, no omelette for breakfast today. You'll have to eat cold cooked potatoes instead.'

'Very well, go and get them.' Watching the door he let himself down from the straw, walked over to the tank of cooked potatoes and threw them up to me, enough for the two of us to share.

'You'd better save some for later', Karol warned, 'in case we can't go down for any more for a while.'

We decided to stay in the barn and get some more sleep, We wanted to get some rest before continuing our journey. 'It will be hard for us to walk in the daytime if we haven't got proper clothes', I said.

'It's no good worrying about that now', Karol said. 'Let's think about that tomorrow.' And we went off to sleep.

In the morning Karol woke me: 'We're going to have omelettes for breakfast. This time I beat the farmer in collecting the eggs and I got some more potatoes too.' We lived on the boiled potatoes and raw eggs for another three days.

On what was perhaps our third morning at the farm a little German boy opened the door of the barn and walked into the stable carrying the egg basket. He went over to the chicken cage to collect the eggs but he was too late: Karol had already taken them. He still looked underneath the chickens but with no success. He shook his head and walked out. Karol and I looked at each other and smiled.

A couple of minutes later the door opened again and the little boy was back with the old German man behind him. 'Father', the boy said, 'I think someone's stealing the eggs.'

Karol sneezed. The old man and the little boy looked at the straw where we were lying but they seemed not to take any notice. The man put his arm around the boy's shoulders and walked him out of the stable.

It wasn't long before I heard the door creak open followed by a shot into the straw and a loud German voice: 'Whoever is hiding there, come out with your hands up, before I kill you!'

Karol and I stood up with our hands in the air and jumped down from the straw. The German laughed: 'Ha, two murderers from the concentration camps! Now I imagine a medal will be waiting for me down at the police station for recapturing you two.'

Each time the old man moved I heard his right foot squeak, but I wasn't sure why until he moved again and I spotted his artificial leg. 'Will that medal really be worth it?', I asked. 'Didn't you get the Iron Cross for losing your leg in the war?' I was very abrupt; we had nothing to lose.

'Never mind about the Iron Cross, you murderers!', yelled the old farmer.

'You call us murderers but we are innocent people who have been taken away from our parents and our homes and put into these striped uniforms and into slave labour camps.'

With his shotgun pointing at us the man marched us out of his farm and into the street, Karol and I leading the limping German and his son. We had walked about a quarter of a mile when we heard aeroplanes overhead. They were hundreds of them. As they got nearer I shouted: 'That's the Russian Air Force!' To Karol I whispered: 'Quick, you shout it's the English Air Force!'

The German and his son looked up. He shouted angrily: 'That is the German Air Force!' The man and his son kept looking and shouting into the sky. I pulled Karol by his arm, managing to escape over a small wall into a garden. We found the garden was actually a cemetery.

We ran for miles without stopping or looking back until we

got near a big town (I don't remember which one). Now at walking pace and able to catch his breath, Karol said: 'I hope we're not taking any chances by walking to the town in these clothes.'

'Don't be silly. You know it's impossible to walk through the streets in these uniforms.'

'We'll have to try our best to break into one of the German houses and get some clothes', Karol insisted.

'That means we'll have to stay here until it gets dark.' But I soon changed my mind: 'Let's go, whatever's going to happen might as well happen now.'

We made our way towards the town, cautiously and silently, until we came to a long street. Hiding in a doorway, we looked around to see which house we should break into to steal some clothes. Just as we stepped out of the doorway a woman and two boys on bicycles came out of a courtyard from the house opposite.

'This is the chance we've been waiting for', I said, and we ran across to the house. We tried the doors; they were locked. We looked all around the house until we found a bathroom window half-open. I squeezed through the tiny opening. Once inside I was able to unlock the bottom part of the window to enable Karol to crawl through.

We couldn't find anything downstairs so we went upstairs. In the bedroom we tried the wardrobe but it was locked. I looked for shoes under the bed and discovered a big trunk; it too was locked. We forced it open and found a suit which would fit either of us and a Hitler Youth uniform. We took them both with two pairs of shoes and socks, pushed the trunk back under the bed and ran downstairs.

In the kitchen Karol took half a loaf of bread and a bottle of milk. We left the house the same way as we came in. We hid in the coal shed in the courtyard while we changed our clothes.

'Which of us is going to wear that uniform?', I asked Karol. 'You wear it.'

'No, you wear it. Oh, what's the difference who's going to wear it as long as we get out of the German territory?' Karol took off his prison clothes and put the suit on. The trousers were short but fitted perfectly. I put on the Hitler Youth uniform, which also had shorts for trousers, but they had to be worn with long socks.

'Now you look like the perfect German!', Karol joked.

'Yes, sir', I said with a *'Heil Hitler!'* salute and we both laughed.

We buried the prison clothes under the coal pile and went freely into the busy city centre. Whenever I saw a German officer walking towards us I made the *'Heil Hitler!'* salute; each of them saluted back with a smile. We wanted to get to the train station but I didn't know which way to go. I asked a soldier on a motorbike in my best German.

'Certainly, the first turning on the right, you can't miss it.' He didn't suspect a thing. I saluted *'Heil Hitler!'* and he replied in kind.

The station was packed with German soldiers and there were German police outside. I didn't want to take a chance and walk through where they were standing so we went in through a little door next to the station and on to the platform. The station was so busy, it looked like no one knew where they were going.

A voice from a loudspeaker announced: 'Next train – Berlin.' Karol was frantic. 'That isn't the way we want to go!'

'God knows how long we'll have to wait for another train!' As the train for Berlin pulled out of the station there was a second announcement: 'The next train is for Warsaw.'

The train for Warsaw came in on the opposite platform. Before we could cross over to the other side, the soldiers had occupied all the seats, and Karol and I had to stand.

11 · Return to Auschwitz

At the first stop I looked through the window and all I could see were German women and children sitting on their luggage waiting for trains going in the opposite direction. The door of the train opened and two tall men in black shiny raincoats – Gestapo men in plain clothes – boarded, pushing their way to the other side of the carriage. They began to question some of the civilian passengers.

When they came back to the end of the carriage where Karol and I were standing they stared at me then opened the door to leave the carriage. One of the men turned to look at me again. He was looking at my shaven hair. 'I am a Gestapo officer. Please let me see your travel documents.'

'I haven't got any. I didn't know I needed any', I replied, shrugging my shoulders.

Unsympathetically he said: 'I am sorry, that's not the answer I want from you. You will have to accompany me to our headquarters.'

'Yes, sir.' We got off the train. Karol and I exchanged frightened glances and we walked down the platform between the two Germans. They took us to an office at the station where a man was sitting at a desk typing. They whispered something to him, then left. The man stared at Karol and said to him: 'Why is your hair shaved off?'

I felt that this time we had no chance of escape. Now he was asking the second question: 'Why haven't you any travel documents?'

I unbuttoned the shirt sleeve on my left arm. 'I have no answers to your questions. Probably this number on my arm will tell all you want to know about us. We have escaped from Auschwitz concentration camp. That is all we have to say for ourselves. You can do what you want with us now.'

He said: 'It is a serious offence for an escaped prisoner to dress in a Hitler Youth uniform.'

'I know your German law very well. So take us out and shoot us like rats against the wall and leave us lying there for weeks without being buried as an example for others!'

'Exactly as you say. But I have to talk it over with the two other Gestapo men when they return and then we will decide what to do with you. In the meantime, I'll have to lock you in the cellar.'

We were led down a few stairs into a dark cellar and the door was locked behind us. Karol began to cry: 'This is the end of our hope to survive.'

I wanted to cheer him up even though I felt the same. 'Don't worry', I said. 'We've got years ahead of us. We can still come out of this alive.' I wasn't sure I believed it myself, but my only thought was to survive in order to meet up with my parents and the rest of my family some day.

We sat there for about an hour until someone came for us. As we walked up the stairs to the station office Karol said: 'This is it, this is the end', accepting a judgment that had not yet been passed.

In the office four Gestapo men stood, glaring at us. Finally one of them spoke: 'We have decided.'

'I know your decision', I yelled, 'to have us shot.'

'You are wrong. We have decided to send you back to Auschwitz.' We had been free for about a week.

I couldn't believe we were lucky enough to get out of that alive. God only knew what would happen to us now.

Karol and I were escorted back by two Gestapo men to the train station to be returned to Auschwitz. We all got on the train and sat down. One of the men took out a packet of cigarettes, and offered me one.

'*Nein, danke schön*', I answered. Of course I smoked, everybody smoked, but I wouldn't take one. They lit their cigarettes and talked about sending parcels home to their families.

From the train we had to walk about two miles along a road lined with guards accompanied by Alsatians. Having reached the camp, we walked on until we arrived outside a guard room – the very place from which Karol and I had escaped.

The Gestapo men knocked on the guard-room door and we

heard a voice from inside: 'Come in.' One of the Gestapo men walked in first, Karol and I behind him; the other Gestapo man shut the door behind us. The SS guard sitting by the desk was drinking coffee from a flask. He nearly choked when he saw our faces. One of the Gestapo men handed him a letter: 'I am leaving these two prisoners in your care. We have to catch the next train back.'

The SS man was Hahn, who had helped us escape. He walked around the room in a daze: 'My God! How did they catch you?' Before I could answer, he opened the letter. 'These two men who brought you here are the German secret service. You're very lucky to be alive and that they brought you back. Now the report tells me I should hand you over to the chief commandant of the camp and strict enquiries should be made as to how you got out of the camp. I've got no more time now as my duty finishes in 15 minutes.' He paused in bewilderment: 'I've got some old prison uniforms lying here in the cupboard. You'd better hurry and put them on before anybody comes in.'

We changed into the striped uniforms and the old guard threw the civilian clothes into the oven. 'I'm going to do the same with the report', he added. 'But remember, not a word to anyone, or you'll get me shot. You'd better hurry out of here. I've got another five minutes before I'm relieved of duty and can forget everything.' He opened the door to the camp and we walked back to our barracks – back into Auschwitz.

We had only been there a few minutes when the camp bells rang for roll call. One of the SS men who were checking us asked: 'Which of you prisoners here come from a different block?' No one answered. He told everyone to show the number tattooed on their arms. The numbers were correct.

When the bells signalling the end of roll call rang, a group of SS men, carrying rifles on their shoulders, surrounded the barracks. An officer ordered us to strip to the waist. While we were undressing, a German officer with two guards and a large Alsatian dog went into the space between two barracks and a third guard followed. The officer sat down in a padded chair. He lit a cigar and his dog sat next to him. 'Are you ready to carry on with the selection?'

'Yes, sir', replied an officer.

'Let's begin.'

The officer instructed us how to walk past the seated man. As each prisoner passed, the officer called out 'Left' or 'Right'. I knew whoever went to the left was condemned to the gas chambers. I also knew that the officer was looking for strong men.

When I passed in front of the officer I had to turn first to face him and then turn my back on him like a model in a dress shop. 'To the right', he said. Next was Karol and he hardly looked at him, but said simply 'To the left'.

I walked to the right to join the group I had been selected for. The rumour went around that the selection officer was a doctor by the name of Mengele. He was supposed to be an experimental doctor, but our group had never heard of him. All I could think about was that after all this time I had lost my brother.

Each group was sent off to separate barracks. I looked around and saw two young boys talking. One was crying. I heard him say: 'They took my brother away from me and he's the only one I have left from all my family. Now this dirty rat has separated us.'

'Listen', I interrupted, 'it's no good crying. The same thing just happened to me. We'll have to do something to get them out of the barracks they were taken to.'

'I guess you're right. If I know it will help to risk my life to get my brother out I will, or we're going to die together in there.'

'Wait until everything's over. I'm going to risk my life the same as you. But don't say a word to anybody.'

'I won't if I know you're going to help me.'

'Don't talk silly, I can't help you.'

'What do you mean?', he asked, puzzled.

'When it comes to it you'll have to help yourself', I said. 'You keep away from me and I'll keep away from you. But we have to watch each other so that when the time comes I will find you and you will find me.' He didn't know what was on my mind.

I walked to the other end of the barracks and sat on the ground close to the guards, watching the back door. It was padlocked. I was sitting, planning how I could get my brother out. The SS were guarding the condemned prisoners at the back and the front of the barracks, so there was only one way. I'd have to go to the little window with iron bars over it facing me and tell Karol how to get out.

As I was thinking, the selection parade finished. Mengele, with his two bodyguards, walked away and the *Kapo* took over: 'Everybody stand in threes! You will march to the table and give the numbers on your arms to the prison clerk.'

As we formed into threes the boy who had his brother in the barracks ran to me and said: 'What are we going to do?'

'Come with me', I said. We ran behind the barracks to the back door; no one was guarding it. When the boy saw the padlock on the door he started crying.

'It's locked! We can do nothing, I've lost my brother after all!'

'Shut up, you fool! Give me that stone, quick!', I yelled. As he handed me a stone, I set the lock in position and with the first bang it opened. I opened the door and all the condemned prisoners ran out. I took Karol by the hand and pulled him after me. We rushed to the table. 'Go in front of me and lift your sleeve up and give your number.' He gave his number, then I gave mine. As we passed the table one of the guards in front of the barracks rushed around to the back and fired a shot in the air to stop the rest of the prisoners from getting in the line.

Two guards formed us into threes again and we were marched to the baths for a hot shower. It took about half an hour and we were ushered out through a different door into a hall. Everybody was fitted out with a new striped suit, hat, shirt and clogs. When everybody was dressed we marched back to the barracks again.

12 · Transfer to Jaworzno

It was January 1943. One morning an SS man walked in shouting: 'Everybody quiet and listen!' It was so quiet you could hear a pin drop. 'Tomorrow morning all of you here will be transferred from Auschwitz to the working camp of Jaworzno to work in the coal mines. If you work hard you will be treated like regular workers and will have everything your heart desires.'

Then he called out: 'I want 12 volunteers to collect your bread and soup from the kitchen.' He had too many volunteers so he counted out 12 men and the rest had to sit down again. Everybody was quiet, waiting for the minute the bread and soup arrived.

It didn't take long. The barracks doors swung open and the men, led by the SS guard, walked in with containers of hot soup and black bread. 'Everybody line up!' We were all given a tin dish. There were four prisoners with soup ladles dishing out a bowl of soup and half a loaf of bread each. We ate like a pack of hungry wolves.

I saw prisoners, under the supervision of the SS guard, pick up their empty containers and get more soup. Everyone was getting as much as they could eat and I felt full up. We were a bit happier, because we knew, for the time being at least, that we were going to work and would avoid the gas chambers.

Soon we heard shouting: 'Everybody quiet!' It was the SS guard: 'Well, how do you feel now after your good food?' Some of the prisoners shouted back: 'Wonderful, sir!'

'That's good', he said and walked out.

'Who's going to give us a song to keep us in shape?', someone shouted. Everybody was feeling happy at the party we were having but afraid to say anything. 'If no one else feels happy, I do,' I said. Right away I had support: 'That's right, we've been selected not to die. So let's have a nice quiet song and we'll be a little happier.'

I sang a song I had heard a few days earlier that suited our situation:

> Tell me where can I go, there's no place I can see.
> Where to go, where to go?
> Every door is closed for me, to the left, to the right,
> It's the same in every land.
> There's nowhere to go and it's me who should know,
> Won't you please understand?
> But I know where I'd like to go,
> Where my folks will proudly stand.
> Where to go, where to go?
> To that precious promised land.
> No more left, no more right,
> Lift my head and see the lights.
> Now you know what I mean,
> That at last if I could be free,
> There will be no more wandering for me.

Many of the prisoners joined in. When we had finished we heard applause. It was an SS man listening through the window. 'What a nice song!', he said, not realizing we had been singing in Yiddish, and he handed me a packet of cigarettes. I took them and he wanted me to carry on singing but I wouldn't. I shared the cigarettes with the rest of the prisoners, breaking each in half to make them go further; but there weren't enough for everyone, so each of us took a few puffs and passed them on.

Eventually the *Stubenälteste* came in and shouted: 'Everybody keep quiet and get to sleep!' We snuggled down together and went to sleep.

During roll call the following morning trucks with open trailers arrived to take us to the work camp. 'Everybody keep your sleeve up and be prepared to show your number', an officer shouted. Each prisoner was checked before he jumped on to a trailer. When the officer checked my number he told me to stay to one side. Everybody was checked and standing in the trailer ready to leave when the SS officer came over to me and said: 'I haven't got your number on the list here.'

'You should have my number on the list because I was picked for this work group.'

'What's your number?' I wanted to lift my sleeve but he said: 'No. Tell me your number without looking at your arm.'

'B4258.'

'That is correct. Let me look at your arm again.' When he looked he said: 'That was my mistake.'

'Well, sir', I said. 'That's not my fault. It is the fault of the prisoner who tattooed my number.'

'Well, it's too late to look into the matter now, I will just have to let you go with that working group.'

'Thank you, sir,' I said and jumped up on the trailer.

There were whistles and shouts. 'Everything ready?'

'Yes sir, yes sir', replied the SS man. He jumped on the first truck and, with the others following, we started to move. We drove through gate after gate until we reached the road. We were standing on the trailers, holding on to each other so close you couldn't get a hair between us. We also had to make room on the back of the truck for the SS men who were guarding us.

For every mile we travelled, the less smoke we could see and smell from the crematoria. We felt happy to be away from the death camp and the gas chambers. We travelled through the high street of the small town of Auschwitz, passing Polish civilians going about their daily business. About an hour later we reached Jaworzno. The barbed wire looked very much like Auschwitz. We stopped just inside the camp gates. The SS officer in command shouted: 'No one is to get off these trailers until you are told to do so.'

A few minutes later a different group of SS guards took charge of us and ordered us to get off the trailers and form into threes to be marched into the disinfectant baths.

It was freezing cold and it had just started to snow. The officer in charge counted 20 prisoners at a time to go into the shower. We were a working party of 600 or 700 prisoners and I was at the end of the line. When it was my turn to step into the showers, we had to undress in a big hall leaving our prison clothes behind us. Inside there were 20 showers hanging from pipes on the ceiling and a cold cement floor with a drain in the middle. The water was nice and warm and it probably saved our lives because we were frozen right through.

The water suddenly went cold and everybody jumped to one side. Just as the water turned hot again we heard a siren and shouting in the camp. The showers stopped, all the lights in the camp went out and everything went quiet. All I could hear was gunfire in the distance. We stood in the shower, naked and wet, while the temperature inside began to drop. Frost began to build up on the window, making patterns like ice flowers. But we couldn't get out of the shower. We had to stay there until the alarm was over. All we could do was press ourselves close together, body to body, to keep warm. We stood there until morning.

At dawn the siren went off and the lights came on all around the camp. The SS men returned and ordered us into the next room to pick up our clothes. Three men lay next to each other on the cold stone floor. An SS man kicked one of them. 'Get up!' There was no answer. They had frozen to death.

I ran outside, naked, with my clothes over my arm. We had to run right across the camp in the freezing snow to get to our barracks. When I had dressed I saw bunks covered with blankets. I couldn't believe these were for the prisoners.

An SS man came in with a *Kapo* and shouted: 'Everybody keep quiet and listen. You are in the Jaworzno camp from which you'll be going to the coal mine to work in three shifts. If you work hard, you'll be looked after. You'll get plenty of food here and more if you want it. You have here in the camp a canteen where you can get cigarettes and extra bread and margarine every month. This prisoner here is going to be the manager of your barracks and, if there is any complaint about new shoes, shirts or uniforms, just report to him and you'll get everything you need.'

Our *Kapo* was a little German man with a hump on his back. He only spoke German and he took to me because he thought I was German too. He tried to show his authority by hitting people all the time, and he could be quite vicious. But we weren't that scared of him; there were *Kapos* a lot bigger than he was.

We all wore the same striped prison uniform, except where I had a red triangle with a P inside for political prisoner, the *Kapo* had a number and a green triangle and a D for *Deutschland*. The green triangle meant he had been a murderer and in prison before the war.

The SS men and the *Kapo* returned to the barracks with new tin basins and spoons for everyone. They brought churns of piping hot soup. The *Kapo* ordered each of us to take a basin and spoon and line up to get our soup and bread. One at a time we went in front of the churns and the *Kapo* poured the thick soup into our basins and filled them right to the top. There were even long wooden tables where we could sit and enjoy our food. The *Kapo* walked between the tables looking at the prisoners' faces, making sure everyone had enough to eat. When we had finished he shouted: 'Everybody outside for inspection!' We rushed out and formed ourselves into threes.

Our *Kapo* trained us how to take off our hats. He explained that the tallest prisoners should always stand at the back and the smallest prisoners should be at the very front. 'When the SS officer arrives,' he told us, 'I am going to say "Attention" and then, when I say "Hats!", all of you quickly, at the same time, reach with your right hands, holding them ready on your heads. Then when I say "Hats off!" you take your hats off, banging them against your right thigh. Everybody must do this at exactly the same second. Everything I told you has to be done at the exact same moment.'

The SS officers were coming towards our barracks so the *Kapo* gave the command 'Hats!' followed by 'Hats off!' And the way we took our hats off, all in the same second like he wanted, was quite impressive. He reported to the officer: 'Sir, 450 prisoners are standing here at attention ready for you to inspect.' The officer wrote something in his book and walked away. But we still couldn't move until the camp bell rang to signal the end of roll call. Then we made our way back to our barracks and lay on the bunks.

The *Kapo* gave an order for everyone to get off their bunks: 'Now I'm going to give you a little demonstration about your beds and your blankets. Everybody has two blankets. When I come in here at night to inspect you when you're asleep, don't let me find one prisoner covered with three blankets and another covered with one blanket. Don't let me catch any prisoner pulling off blankets from other prisoners while they're asleep, because if I find out, or if it is reported to me that anyone is taking blankets from the others, there will be a heavy penalty to pay. You are not in a holiday camp here. This is the Jaworzno labour camp. Whatever you are told to do, must be done. You understand me?

'Now I'm going to show you how to make your beds. When you wake up in the morning half an hour before roll call, which will be at 5.30, here is how to make your beds. They must be straight as a board. Put your blankets together, throw them over the bed, tuck them under each side of the straw mattress and smooth them out with your hands on top. There mustn't be any creases. It's not up to me. It's up to SS Officer Lausman, who comes to inspect the barracks, to see if they are clean and tidy. If not, you'll be out of work. As you can see, every bed has its own number and you'd better remember the number of your bed. If the bed hasn't been made the way I told you, the SS man will take the number of the bed and you'll be punished. Is that clear?'

Everyone began to experiment in making their own beds until they were made according to the *Kapo*'s orders.

The next morning the camp bells rang for roll call. We stood in threes as usual. This time about 40 SS officers with rifles attended roll call. But instead of being dismissed after roll call, the command was 'Left turn, forward march!' until we got to the camp gate. Then the SS officer in charge shouted: 'Company, halt! Now you see this gate here. Every time you march in or out you will shout in a loud voice "Good luck!"' And then he shouted 'Company, attention! Company, march!' As we went past the gate all of us shouted 'Good luck!'.

The officer walked from one side of the group to the other, making sure all the prisoners marched straight like soldiers, 'left, right, left, right'. The SS men walked by the side of us pointing their rifles at us, pushing anyone who didn't walk in time and shouting 'That's the way you should march – left, right, left, right'.

We continued like this until we got to a lift at the coal mine. 'Company, halt! Right turn!' A group was counted out and went into the lift. One lift went down full of prisoners and one lift came up empty. I was in the next group to go into the coal mine and as I went further underground I began to feel warmer and warmer.

The lift stopped and I got out and looked around – I had come to a different world. I only had the chance to go a few yards because there were Polish civilian coal miners sorting out the prisoners, as they arrived, into departments inside the mine.

I was put to work at the mine placing dynamite in small holes in the walls. Later I was transferred to group number six, the train department. I worked as an apprentice, under a civilian supervisor, on the electric train. Karol was given the job of coupling the train wagons. We brought the coal up from where other prisoners were mining the coal. My supervisor told me that British prisoners-of-war had been working there before we came.

'What happened to them?', I asked.

'They've been returned to their camps and aren't sent out to work any more. All you and I have to do', he explained, 'is to collect all the trucks that have been filled up with coal and bring them back to the lift and wait until it goes to the top. Now another thing: I've got an electric torch and I have to teach you all the signals so that we understand each other. Sometimes I have to bring very long trains up. You will be right at the back sitting on the last truck, and you must make sure that a truck doesn't break away from the others. If it does, blow the whistle and flash your torch on and off and then I will know I have to stop everything.'

When I'd finished my first day's work, I sat down close to the lift until all the prisoners had assembled from the different parts of the coal mine. As we went up in the lift, the second-shift prisoners were ready to go down. We were marched across the road to the showers and told to wash very well because we were to be inspected.

We stood naked, ready to be inspected by SS officer Lausman – an absolute madman. Sometimes he could make a joke with a prisoner and sometimes, when he was in a bad mood, he would punish them. When Lausman came in to inspect the prisoners we all stood to attention. He looked at my neck and ears. Then he turned to look at an old man standing next to me. He decided that the old man's ears were not clean enough and pulled him to one side. He called me out of the line and handed me a stick: 'You give him 15 lashes across the back and I will stand here and count the blows.'

I had no choice; I hit the old man while Lausman counted. But I was barely touching his body and I didn't hurt him. I had given him six lashes when Lausman pulled the stick from my hand. 'You dog, that isn't the way to hit! Not the way I mean! I will show you how it should be done!' He struck me across the back: 'Can you feel that?'

I straightened my back and looked at him, but gave no response. This made him angry. He hit the old man until he collapsed at the eleventh lash. Lausman reminded us at the top of his voice that if we were at any time found dirty we would receive the same punishment, if not worse: 'Now you have five minutes to get dressed!'

When we were dressed we hurried outside and formed into rows of threes. Right away we were surrounded by SS guards and checked to see no one was missing. Lausman commanded: 'Right turn, forward march!' As we marched back to the camp, the old man shuffled along in front of me. He could hardly walk. The two prisoners next to him saw him stumbling; they knew he couldn't march but they were too cowardly to help him. One of the other prisoners and I changed places with these cowards, determined to help the poor old man.

Lausman saw what happened but didn't say anything. He counted the steps slowly with a grin on his wicked face until we reached the camp gates. Again he shouted 'Company halt, one, two!' and we were checked in again by the chief officer of the camp.

Each prisoner gave the 'Good luck!' shout and was dismissed. My friend and I took the old man to the camp hospital where he was detained by the doctors. We rushed back to the barracks and ate our meal as if it might be our last. Then we lay on our bunks for an hour and a half until the door was thrown open and an SS guard walked in shouting '*Achtung!*'

We all jumped up from the bunks when Lausman walked in and began: 'I was here this morning to inspect your bunks. I found them very untidy. I have taken the numbers of the beds which were most untidy – 130 and 181. I'm not going to punish these two separately but I will punish all of you and you will know next time. Everybody on your bunks! Now down! Now up! Now down!'

This carried on for about half an hour until the younger

prisoners made it clear to the officers that they saw it as a joke. The more we laughed the angrier Lausman became. He carried on and on with his so-called punishment. After some time, when the commander called out for us to get up on to our bunks, I jumped up to my top bunk, conveniently forgot to come down and fell asleep. When I woke up it was all over and I found all the prisoners laughing and joking.

The next day we were again woken at five o'clock by the camp bells and were given some black coffee to drink before going to work. Then the procedures of the previous day were repeated. This was our routine, day in day out.

One morning we went through roll call, then were counted again and then again. One prisoner was missing. We were made to stand for hours while a search ensued. In the corner of the camp new barracks were being built for prisoners arriving at Jaworzno. At first no one thought of searching there for the missing prisoner. When they eventually looked there, they found the prisoner hanging by the neck from his own belt behind a stack of boards.

About a week later I was transferred to the afternoon shift at the coal mines. By this time it was almost summer 1943. I remember one day lying on the sand behind the barracks with some other prisoners. The weather was baking hot. Suddenly we heard a warning siren from the camp. Five minutes after the siren stopped we heard firing from the anti-aircraft guns. We saw small clouds of smoke from the bursting shells. There were hundreds of heavy bombers but we didn't know whose planes they were. They were shining like stars and we thought this might be the beginning of the end. We stood there, looking up, and I could tell by the other prisoners' faces that they were thinking the same as me.

All of a sudden we heard two large explosions and the camp filled with smoke; it was hard for us to see each other. All the prisoners in the camp began to shout: 'We would sooner get killed by our friends dropping bombs than get shot in the back by you dirty rats!' Meaning the SS, of course. Soon the smoke cleared and it became evident that not one of the SS guards was to be seen around the camp.

When it was safe to look around I saw that the kitchen and

food storage room at the main entrance of the camp had been hit. There was chaos as the prisoners swarmed around, looting all the food they could salvage. We thought the Germans had disappeared and abandoned us, but we were mistaken. Shots were heard and there was shouting and gunfire as the prisoners scrambled back to their barracks.

The prisoners began bartering with each other. Those with margarine swapped it for a slice of bread and those with bread exchanged it for marmalade. This went on for weeks. In one part of the barracks there was a proper bazaar; two prisoners watched in case any SS men came near the barracks. The bazaar became popular in the camp. When the prisoners got their dinner they would go there to barter. Once I walked in and saw prisoners standing by their bunks; one was holding a bowl of piping hot soup, the other a slice of salami. Some of the prisoners would even trade their own prison clothes. If some prisoners, who never went out of the camp to work, had a new uniform, they would exchange it with a prisoner who worked in the coal mines. The mine workers had to promise half of their dinner in exchange for the clothes. We were all getting used to each other and to the camp.

When we worked below in the coal mines some of the prisoners would rush to finish their work in eight hours. If they didn't finish it in that time they would be held back for another shift.

Prisoners would tease one another: 'Ah, Sam. Why you rushing with your work? Do you think you'll be late for the cinema?'

'He's got to meet his girlfriend tonight', someone said.

We prisoners who worked so hard, with sweat pouring down our bodies, never lost hope of being free again. This is how we lived our miserable lives, slaving for the Germans.

Winter was coming around again and we began to hear interesting stories from the civilians in the coal mine, to the effect that the Russian front was getting nearer and nearer to Jaworzno city and camp. The prisoners didn't care what was happening and regarded even a true story as a tale. Then that tale became reality.

13 · Death March to Blechhammer

One morning around November–December 1943 the night shift returned from the mines but the morning shift wasn't allowed out of the camp. We were kept there all day doing nothing. When the afternoon shift too was held back, we knew something unusual was happening. There wasn't even an inspection throughout the day. We heard a bell ring and shouts over the camp loudspeaker: 'Everybody go to your barracks and go to sleep. You'll be woken up at four o'clock in the morning. Wrap up your blankets and carry them across your backs. You're going on a long march.'

At four in the morning every single prisoner in the camp was up and we formed ourselves into threes. As we stood waiting for further instructions, it began to snow. More orders came: 'You will now march out. One barracks of prisoners will follow the next. Don't let anyone think of stopping and hiding anywhere because this camp will be burned down later in the day.' A pause was followed by the order: 'SS men, be ready to take command over the prisoners! *Heil Hitler!*'

We marched column after column out of the gate, five or six prisoners at a time. The *Kapo* with the hump had disappeared overnight. We marched through towns and villages, heavily guarded by SS guards. We must have walked some 40 miles that day. When night fell we stopped in a town, dead tired and hungry. Whoever had a slice of bread was considered as rich as a millionaire, but no one had a bed to sleep in.

Each time we stopped, we noticed that half of the SS guards went to sleep while the others guarded us. We were being treated worse than animals. We had been standing in the cold darkness for hours when we saw the guards coming back to change shifts. We all spread our blankets on the icy road to lie down to sleep. Just as I was settling down I heard shouts: 'Everyone on your feet!' I stood up and tried to pick my blanket up off the ground, but it was useless: it had frozen to the road. We resumed our march. This time we marched day and night without stopping.

Whenever we approached a town our SS guards would direct us towards fields and forests. They would shout 'Quick, keep moving!' and we would run faster and faster. Those who couldn't run were shot in the back of the head. Blood spurted all over the pure white snow.

The guards kept on shooting at prisoners who couldn't keep up; eventually they were firing on all the prisoners from behind. They just kept on killing, for no reason at all. The prisoners at the back pushed to the front to avoid being shot. We ran like wild animals, terrified. The more we ran, the more excited the SS became, shrieking 'Get going! Get going!' and firing again and again into the crowd.

The blood ran like a river along the road. And they called us gangsters! It is almost impossible to believe that such people as these SS guards existed, so ruthless and cold-blooded. They were like monsters from another planet. We suffered terribly at their hands. All we could do was hope that that day or the next the war would be over. Meanwhile, we had to keep on marching.

One night when the air was thick with snow we reached a forest, marching through falling snow that came right up to our thighs. Through the snow we saw in the sky what looked like flashes of lightning. We heard heavy shells whistle over our heads, then we heard the explosions and we knew we had run into the front line.

When the SS men saw the explosions and flashes of light they again shouted 'Get going! Get going!' Anyone unable to keep up or with frozen feet was shot. They kept us marching while the number of prisoners fell constantly. We marched like this for about three weeks without any proper food or water. All we ate was snow. Whenever we marched through a town and a prisoner spotted a dustbin outside a door he would rush to it in a desperate search for something to eat.

The Germans wouldn't shoot prisoners in the streets, where they could be seen by civilians. They watched us – not marching but crawling along, starving and exhausted. Some of us didn't even have wooden clogs on our feet, just pieces of blanket tied around them. The civilians stood and watched us as if they couldn't care less who we were or where we were going. But as soon as we had marched a few miles away from the town the SS men opened fire again killing more prisoners.

Then we stopped. The guards formed us into threes, telling some of the prisoners to remove their blankets from around their necks: 'This march finishes tomorrow morning and you must all look at least a little presentable. Tomorrow we are marching into a camp where you'll get food and rest.'

We marched all night until we reached a forest. Then we saw barracks with pieces of broken glass fixed on top. We stopped outside the camp and collapsed on the icy road, half-dead. We lay there for about half an hour before the SS started shouting again: 'On your feet!' I hardly knew what they meant by 'On your feet!' – I had no feet left. I felt I could just about crawl along until we got inside the camp. This was Blechhammer, some 20 miles from Leipzig. It was now the beginning of 1944.

Immediately we were inside the camp, we lined up in the kitchen for a bowl of soup and two slices of bread each. We couldn't eat it fast enough before we were rushing into the barracks looking for a place to lie down. I don't think anyone in the world could have moved us off those bunks, even if we knew we were going to be killed. We made ourselves comfortable and fell into an exhausted sleep.

I was woken up abruptly by one of the resident prisoners: 'Did you hear the orders through the loudspeakers?'

'No', I croaked, barely able to speak.

'All prisoners who were in this camp before and all prisoners who don't want to carry on marching can stop here.'

Then I heard the loudspeaker myself: 'If you want to march we will have to shift all you prisoners out of here immediately as the Russian front line is getting closer.'

I couldn't believe what this prisoner was telling me. 'Are you one of the long-term prisoners in this camp?', I asked him.

'Yes', he said, 'I've been here for months.'

'What are you prisoners going to do?', I asked. 'Are you going to march or are you going to stay here?'

'We'll have to march.'

'March!', I exploded. 'You don't know what marching is!

99

I've been marching for three weeks until we got here! This is our only stop after three weeks to have a bit of food and rest. If you're stupid and go with them you'll just suffer the same as I did. As we were marching they were shooting us in the back for no reason at all. So, if I have to march again and get shot in the back, I'd sooner die lying here on this bunk with my brother.'

'You're probably right. But I don't want to take any chances. God knows what they're going to do with the prisoners who stay here.'

Then there were whistles and shouts: 'Whoever is marching, leave the camp immediately!' The prisoner to whom I was talking made up his mind and rushed out.

'What are we going to do, Karol?', I asked, already knowing what his reply would be.

'I couldn't march any longer even if I wanted to', he moaned. 'Whatever's going to happen, let it happen here.' We didn't need any further discussions. On the other side of the barracks were a number of prisoners who felt the same as we did.

'How many of us are in this barracks?' We counted nine. 'It's no good us sitting here together. Let's hide separately under different bunks in case they take a look in.' Karol and I went to a corner of the barracks, broke the boards from under a bunk and lay underneath them, wondering what was going to happen next.

We were lying there quietly and the camp seemed deserted when all of a sudden we heard someone shouting: 'Anyone in the barracks, come out! We're free! The SS have gone! The war must be over!' We rushed to the camp square. Prisoners were coming from all directions. There must have been some 700 prisoners leaving through the unguarded camp gates.

Some prisoners were coming back from the railway station not far from the camp smartly dressed. They had found clothes the Germans had left behind. Karol came back with two leather jackets and pushing a brand new motorbike. 'We saw two Russian patrol tanks and they gave us cigarettes', he said. 'If you don't believe me, have a look. I've got some Russian cigarettes!'

'What else did they say?' I wasn't interested in cigarettes. I wanted to know if the war really was over and if we were free to go home. 'One of the soldiers said we should stop where we are. They'll come into our camp soon but they're the only patrol and they have to go back now.' At that moment we heard planes nearby. We saw Russian and German fighters battling it out over our heads. We all rushed back into the camp until everything went quiet again.

Karol and I decided we would scavenge our new camp home for food. We found a stable of sorts next to the SS barracks and opened the door only to find two prisoners inside. One was standing with an axe in his hands and the other was chasing a pig around. As I looked at the prisoners and then at the pig my impression was that the pig was going to kill them – they looked like walking skeletons. I told the two men to stay outside and keep the door shut. I took the axe and struck the pig over the head. I walked out and said to them: 'The rest I'll leave to you and don't forget to save a piece of bacon for me.'

Karol and I took a walk around the camp until we found the prison hospital. There must have been over 100 prisoners in it. Some were lying helpless and crying for joy that the SS had left the camp and the war was over. The more I saw the worse I felt; I couldn't bear seeing these men abandoned and dying for nothing.

I saw a group of prisoners standing around a bonfire, cooking what food they could find in used cans. I walked a bit further on to another group of prisoners who were frying chunks of bacon in a larger discarded can.

A prisoner ran towards us, breathless. 'Lads, lads!', he shouted.

'What are you shouting for? What's wrong?'

'I could swear I saw an SS man with a machine gun closing the gates from the outside', he exclaimed terrified.

Some of the prisoners said: 'You're mad. You don't know what you're talking about. Here, have a chunk of bacon. It will make you feel better.'

But the man was right. Just at that moment we heard machine-gun fire. There was panic throughout the camp: people simply didn't know what was happening. I peeped out through a side window in the barracks I found myself in, and saw prisoners being mowed down as they ran for cover.

Bullets shattered the roof of the barracks; in desperation we ran out of that building into another. Bullets sprayed that building too. We tried to find somewhere to hide.

Just a few yards away was an underground shelter where the Germans kept potatoes in the winter. Prisoners were running towards the shelter, but were being shot before they could reach the door. I saw a guard standing on the wall and holding a machine gun; the gun was pointed at the shelter door and he was firing without let-up. He had killed so many prisoners that the door was blocked by dead bodies.

We ran into one of the barracks. There was a huge explosion. As I looked up I saw pieces of bedding in the prison hospital fly into the air. We ran into another barracks and lay flat on our stomachs on the floor. There was another explosion, this time in the barracks we were in, which began to burn. Again we fled, crossing the yard to another building. Bullets whistled past our ears as we were caught in the crossfire from two sides of the camp.

The camp was lit up by the fire and there was a pall of smoke hanging over everything. We kept running, looking for cover, caught like mice in a trap. I said to one of the prisoners: 'Our time has come to get killed or probably burnt in one of these barracks. If we're going to get killed, let's die fighting. But I've got an idea and I need a few volunteers. If we're lucky we'll probably save ourselves and the other prisoners too. So who's coming with me?'

There was Karol, myself and four Russians. 'Alright', they conceded, 'but what are your plans?'

'Look through the window. Can you see that SS guard firing his machine gun? The six of us have to walk, one after the other, along the other side of the wall next to the guard without him seeing us. As we'll be close to the wall, he won't see us and he'll be firing over our heads into the camp. Then, if we stand on each other's shoulders, two high, we can tear his machine gun out of his hands, which he won't expect. This can easily be done if we're not afraid. Then we make for the gate. You, being a soldier', I said to one of them, 'you must know what to do. Are you ready?'

The four agreed without hesitation. Two of them said a prayer.

We stood under the wall while we planned our next move. One of the lads suddenly fell to the ground and I saw he was covered in blood. He was dead. Bullets were flying everywhere; we didn't know where they were coming from. Karol and the others put their arms around each others' shoulders. I crawled up the human ladder and turned around to face the camp with one leg on my brother's shoulder and one leg on another prisoner. My hands could barely reach the machine gun sticking out over the wall, resting on it. But I managed to grab it with both hands, making sure the weight of my body was strong enough to snatch it from the German.

I gave a jerk, my feet came off the shoulders of the boys below and in one motion I was on the ground with the machine gun in my hands. The German was looking over the wall: 'You dirty dogs!', he exclaimed. I fired in his direction and didn't see him any more.

We ran around by the wall to get to the gate but an SS man saw us and fired. He ducked under the wall as I fired back and when I looked around I saw there were more and more prisoners following us.

There came more shots from the guard, killing more prisoners. I shot back at him; he ducked once again. We ran for the gate and tried to pull it open; it was locked. One of the prisoners shouted: 'Watch it, lads! The German just threw something over the wall.'

I saw a small flat box with a smoking wick. 'Quick, hide!', I shouted. I ran to the box and flung it at the gate. There was an enormous explosion. Pieces of gate flew through the air in all directions. One of the pieces hit me in the face.

I ran into the barracks shouting: 'The gate is destroyed and there are no more German guards outside. Who's coming with me to have a look around!' There were about 50 prisoners ready to come with me. They picked up sticks and wooden bunk-bed legs. As the barracks blazed we walked out through the gate looking in the direction from which the guards had been firing. There was nobody there and the camp seemed to be clear of Germans.

Everything was on fire. The Russians and the Germans were fighting it out in the sky over our heads. The German ground forces were moving in while Russian forces were held up at the base of the mountain where the goods train was. We didn't realize we were in the middle of the front line, but none of us was afraid to die. We ran towards the hill and the Russian troops. The Germans began shooting, killing many prisoners, easy targets in our striped prison uniforms.

The Russian soldiers gave us their machine guns while they rested. They loaded the ammunition magazines into the guns as we fired at the enemy. Some of the Russians gave us bread and corned beef; we ate and fought at the same time. It was a glorious feeling for us concentration-camp prisoners to be in the front line, fighting side by side with Russian troops, firing a machine gun with dignity. I had the power to fight back against the SS army and take revenge for the deaths of so many of the prisoners in the camp.

But our joy didn't last long, for after a few hours of heavy exchange of artillery fire the Russian army pulled back and we were left on our own. One of the prisoners had a pair of binoculars and could see the Germans advancing. We all headed for a goods train at the station where we found boxes of clothes marked 'Essen, Germany'. The clothes were from victims of the gas chambers, probably murdered a few weeks earlier. We broke open the crates and put the civilian clothes over our prison uniforms.

Suddenly there was panic. We ran back to the camp to see prisoners pulling out those who were still alive from the burning hospital barracks. But for some of the prisoners it was too late. They were cremated in the hospital furnace while the remaining prisoners stood by helpless, watching the flames take the bodies high into the sky. All we could do was weep.

We gathered what belongings we had, such as blankets or any other things that might be useful, and walked through the camp gates intending to head for home. Only a few steps away from the camp, as we were heading into the forest, we saw five Russian tanks coming towards us, firing in all directions. The Germans retaliated. Shells exploded all around us. We all ran back to the camp.

The barracks were still ablaze. The Russians may have thought they were responsible for the burning of the camp and the German soldiers may have thought it was their luck to destroy it. In fact, neither was the case. The smouldering barracks were the work of the SS men who had been left behind. They wanted to destroy Blechhammer so that no evidence of their being there would ever be found.

Two SS men were still in the camp, one on each corner of a lookout tower. They had enough fire power to kill the remaining prisoners. There was non-stop machine-gun fire and explosions of hand grenades. The SS were trying to destroy everything.

We fled into one of the barracks that was left standing, running near the fire, through the fire, behind the fire. We couldn't care less where we ran as long as we could hide from the SS. Some of the prisoners were saying: 'We can't get out of here. We're right in the middle of the German–Russian front line. We'd all better hide, quickly, or we'll be killed.'

14 · On the March Again

We hid as quickly as we could and waited to see who would come into the camp first, the Germans or the Russians. If the Germans came first we would stay in our hiding places and if it was the Russians we would come out.

When we looked up at the sky, through the blown-off roof of the barracks, we could see German fighters battling it out with the Russians. Hundreds of empty shells rained down over the camp. Even though we were frightened, we were pleased because we thought it was all going to come to an end and we would be free to go home.

But that wasn't the case. The Russians had been pushed back by the German army. The Germans came into the camp first. I don't know what gave us away but I heard shouting: '*Raus, raus, raus!*' I guess a few men started coming out from their hiding places because we could hear a commotion outside.

It was now dark and we lay silently beneath the bunks we were using for cover. We thought we couldn't be seen and hoped they would think the barracks were empty. Suddenly the Germans shone their torches in our faces. We crawled out from under the bunks, terrified. We knew they would throw hand grenades inside the building to make sure there were no survivors.

We thought we were the only ones left but when we went outside other prisoners began to appear, one by one. The German officers took us all outside the camp gates. One of them asked a soldier: 'How many are there here?'

None of the soldiers knew exactly: 'Quite a few,' the man replied.

By the time we had all gathered together there were some 250 of us left.

'What are we going to do with them?', I overheard one of the lower-ranking soldiers ask an officer.

'We'll take them to a village or town and give them up to the police. Let them deal with them.' The soldiers then marched us into the forest. Opposite our camp we passed a British prisoner-of-war camp, Stalag 8. There was no one left there now either.

The floor of the forest wasn't all that difficult to walk on because the trees caught most of the falling snow. But as soon as we reached an open space the snow was so deep we could hardly walk. We trudged along, pulling our feet out of the snow at every step. The German soldiers were in the same position but they were also carrying backpacks that weighed them down. Eventually they had to pull their feet out of their jackboots and leave them standing in the snow. I smiled inwardly at their predicament.

At one point during the march some of the prisoners broke away from the German soldiers and ran towards the front-line soldiers, whom they recognized from their uniforms – the helmets, machine guns, binoculars and hand grenades that hung from their belts. These prisoners didn't want to live any longer and expected to be shot if they ran away. They simply wanted to give the soldiers an excuse to shoot them down. But the Germans ran after the prisoners and brought them back to the group; they wouldn't shoot anybody. They weren't SS, they weren't Gestapo, they were regular soldiers and we knew from previous experience that regular soldiers didn't behave like the bestial Gestapo.

We marched through the night and arrived at a village the next day. I could tell it was a fairly large village by the size of the church and the cottages. Down the main street, was the town hall and police station. The soldiers made us stop right outside the police station while one of the officers went in to report. A man came out wearing a green uniform – a German gendarme. The gendarmes all came out and stood talking among themselves in the cold for about half an hour. Then they took their bicycles and tied what looked like food parcels on to the saddles with belts. They ordered us to march on.

It was around February 1944. We marched for two or three weeks. But we didn't seem to cover a lot of ground, we just sort of plodded along.

One day a German police corporal who was pushing his

bike alongside me said to me: 'Very cold, isn't it?'

They thought we could only speak Polish but he was wrong in my case. I answered in German: 'Yes, it is. When you get tired I wouldn't mind pushing your bike for you.'

He looked at me with a smile on his face. He carried on looking until finally he said: 'You remind me of my family. I have a son as big as you. He looks a bit like you too.' Every German who looked at me told me that. I hated it.

'Oh yeah? Perhaps I am him!' Unfortunately I wasn't.

'Whenever you want', he said, 'help me with the bike.' Every time after that, when he unloaded his parcel from his bicycle, he gave me a piece of bread. Sometimes he had salami or a carrot. He gave me a bit of salami with the bread once but I spat it out. It could have killed me because it was too fatty and my body wasn't used to that kind of food any more. I had seen prisoners die from eating stolen food that their stomachs couldn't digest.

We carried on trudging through the snow. The policeman looked after me and I kept pushing his bike. One day I saw a factory with a tall chimney in the distance. As we passed the factory a prisoner fell on to a small heap of snow. When he tried to get up, he discovered he had fallen on to a mound of harvested sugar beets. The factory was a sugar factory! But like everything else around there it wasn't working; the factory stood deserted, all snowed up. We all grabbed the sugar beets and the gendarmes couldn't stop us.

There were only a few policeman with us now, but we still were unable to do anything to free ourselves. Even if the prisoners had wanted to kill the police in the fields it would have been of no use. We didn't know where we were or, more importantly, where we were going. We were still alive so we carried on marching.

After another four days or so we passed the factory again and of course we grabbed the sugar beet again. A few days later we passed it again. Then again. About six times we passed the factory. We were marching in circles! 'Why', I thought. 'Why are they taking us in circles? Perhaps they're lost'. I asked the German whose bike I was pushing: 'Tell me, we're not going to survive, are we?'

'Oh, yes', he said. 'Don't worry, everything will be alright.'

'Why are we going around in circles? Why can't you take us somewhere definite – to another camp so at least we would be under shelter?'

'No, no, no, we can't do that', he insisted.

'Haven't you got a destination? Where are we going?'

'If we give you up at the next station or camp, it would make no difference', the German police corporal confessed. 'Then we'd have to report back to base and we don't want to report because where we would be going next is a lot colder than here.'

At that point I realized what was happening. If they turned us in and reported back to their base, they would be sent to the Russian front. He was so terrified at the thought of it that he couldn't even mention that front. Every German soldier was petrified of it: if any officer wanted to punish a lower-ranking soldier he would send him straight to the front line. We even heard of soldiers committing suicide to avoid being sent there.

We marched on through the snow until we came to open roads which had been cleared of snow, making walking a bit easier. We could see a black mass on the road ahead. We got nearer and nearer until we could see that it was a group of British prisoners-of-war marching towards us. The Germans were confused. They didn't know where to take us and they didn't know where to take the British POWs. We marched right past each other.

On we marched, laboriously, not like soldiers, but step by painful step. Then we saw smoke in the distance. As we got nearer the smoke I could see church steeples, buildings and a lot of ruins. As we walked through the burnt-out city we saw a signpost in the ground bearing its name – Leipzig. The entire city was flattened. There wasn't much to see because it had been bombed by the Russian air force. The buildings were just shells without windows or roofs.

We marched right through the city and out the other side, coming to a set of railway tracks. We followed the tracks for three or four miles until we lost sight of Leipzig. We came to a patch of ground that had been cleared of snow with tracks from big, heavy tyres: it could have been trucks or snow ploughs or anything. We were told to stop.

We sat down where the ground was free from ice or snow.

We were so glad to rest. We didn't care if we stopped or walked on, or if we fell asleep and never woke up. We didn't care about anything. There was nothing to eat so we sucked handfuls of snow. We sat there, waiting for a miracle, but nothing happened. The gendarmes got on their bikes and started back towards Leipzig. They said they would come back but they didn't. We sat there a whole day and night, sleeping on the ground, living on snow.

Out of nowhere came trucks with Waffen SS, who guarded the camps, and SS soldiers too. No one said anything; we just sat there until we heard a commotion between the officers and the soldiers. An open cattle train arrived with about six or eight wagons. We were ordered on to the train and sat, wondering what was happening; it was at least 12 hours before we started to move.

If we were doomed to die, this was the day. Still, we didn't completely give up hope. 'Perhaps. Perhaps something's going to happen.' But nothing did.

We were on the train for days, stopping in places we didn't know where. At the stops the SS would turn up with large urns filled with black tea. It was just coloured water, cherry leaves boiled in water, not really tea at all. We didn't care. At least they gave us something and it was warm. We would have our tea and the SS would shut the doors leaving us to sit in silence. No one said anything because there was nothing to say. We didn't know anything, where we were, where we were going, what was happening to us, nothing.

At one point we felt the train sway off the main line and we heard an express train in the distance. We looked over the top of the cattle trucks and saw a German Red Cross train full of wounded soldiers. We didn't know where they were coming from but I guessed they were from the Russian front line on their way to German hospitals. Not far from there we pulled off the main track again and another Red Cross train passed. The express trains kept coming.

After eight or ten days on the train I realized we were in the same situation as when we were marching. They didn't know where to put us or get rid of us. We were lucky we weren't executed in the first forest they could find.

One day on this never-ending journey we passed through a train station enclosed on one side by mountains. As the train crawled through the station I looked to my left and I saw a signpost with the station's name: Dresden. I saw soldiers of all ranks, some carrying packs and some on crutches, gendarmes, several SS men, even civilians with push-chairs packed with their worldly possessions. I guessed they were trying to escape the bombing. I learned later that most of the city had been destroyed, but it was still standing when we passed through it.

15 · Leitmeritz Camp

The train kept moving. It was daylight when we had passed through Dresden and we travelled two more nights. We didn't know what day it was, we didn't even know what year it was. Suddenly we stopped – and luckily for us we did because they had given us no food in those two days. I thought they wanted us to die on the train so it would be easier for them. When we stopped all we could hear was the engine of the train puffing; we sat for about four hours with nothing happening. Then suddenly trucks arrived with SS soldiers and the shouting began: *'Achtung! Achtung! Achtung!'* Almost by rote, we dragged ourselves off the train.

The SS counted us and gave us the order to march. Was it the beginning of another few weeks walking in the snow? Perhaps it was the end for us. God alone knew. The empty trains moved on and we walked slowly for about two hours. Eventually we arrived in a field and saw a big gate. We wondered if it was the crematoria or a camp; we didn't know. On top of the gate was the familiar sign *'Arbeit macht frei'*.

Our new camp was called Leitmeritz. We were near Theresienstadt camp, just north of Prague. It was March or April 1944.

The SS guards let us in and a very large man, our *Kapo*, approached us. His name was Jakob. He wore a three-quarter-length jacket with a woollen scarf on his head like a cap and on his yellow armband was written *Kapo* in old German letters. He marched us into a big shower in one of the barracks. We were very cold and only lukewarm water was coming out of the shower. I was frightened because I had heard they played tricks like this when you went into the shower but never came out. I asked Jacob – after all, what did I have to lose? – 'Is this the end? Is this extermination?'

112

'Don't worry, you'll come out', Jakob said. 'Just have a shower, you'll be out. I promise you.' He was right.

After the shower we collected new striped jackets, trousers and hats from baskets wheeled in on little trolleys. We stood up, were counted again and marched across the camp to an enormous barracks. On each side of the barracks there was a four-tier bunkbed that went right across the room. Jakob motioned to the left side and said we could choose where we wanted to sleep. Karol and I went to the third tier. There was just enough room for all the prisoners.

There was no food yet but we were glad to get some rest. About an hour later the *Kapo* came back and took us to the kitchen. We were each given a can to collect the hot soup and a piece of black bread. We were to keep these cans as our own, to be used for anything that required a container. We were all free to walk about in the camp. We went back to the barracks and lay down with our heads sticking out of the bunks towards the centre of the room.

In the early evening more prisoners arrived. They were prisoners-of-war: Mongolians. They slept in the bunk across from ours on the other side of the barracks. They could only speak Russian, but some of us could speak a little Russian too. They wanted to know where we had come from. We told them about the train and I asked one of them: 'Where have you just come from?'

'We're working', he told me.

'Working where? There's no factory outside.'

'We work in the factory in the camp. When you go out into the camp', he explained, 'you go across the road further down. You'll see sliding iron gates, numbered with white paint.'

'What's that?'

'It's an underground factory. It's like being in a city, with lights and everything.'

'So, are you getting good treatment here?'

'Yes. You'll be alright if you can get work in there.'

'That's probably why I'm here', I answered.

The next day the guards took down our prisoner numbers. (There were never any names, just numbers.) They told us that the following day we would be up at 5.30 to go to work. We didn't feel like going to work but we had to. At 5.30 the next morning a prisoner on top of a guard tower sounded roll call on his trumpet. The day shift was preparing to go out and we could hear the night shift coming in, shuffling their clogged feet along the gravel path. After the night shift had gone to their barracks four *Kapos* came to take us to work.

The doors of the factory were huge and guarded on both sides. When they opened I could see a series of tunnels winding beneath the mountain. Bright lights ran right through the middle of the tunnel system. As I had thought, you could get a tank through the door: this was a parts factory for German tanks.

The components for the machines were brought in from outside and we assembled them in the tunnels. Parts for planes were also assembled in the tunnels. We put the tyres on the aeroplane wheels. We didn't do a lot of work; in fact, we did as little as possible. If there were nuts and bolts to tighten we would never do it properly. The *Kapos* would run up and down to make sure we were working, but the minute they left us, we stopped. We were in no hurry to help build up the German air force.

There were prisoners of all nationalities in Leitmeritz – Poles, Hungarians, Czechs, Russians, Mongolians (as I mentioned) and even about 120 German political prisoners who were in charge of the *Kapos*. You could recognize the German prisoners by the way they were dressed. They wore black uniforms with no insignia, black forage caps and jackboots like the German soldiers, though these were the only military aspects of their uniforms. The German prisoners were also treated better than the other prisoners. Some were there because they were communists; others were common criminals sent to the camps at the beginning of the war.

Those who worked in the factory worked eight-hour shifts, seven days a week. Being workers like we were, the Germans didn't come around to the barracks to check on us very often. They thought we were doing such a good job making the tanks in the mountains that they didn't bother us too much. Little did they know, we were doing just enough to save our lives – they demanded a hundred per cent and we gave about

14. The author (right) with brother Karol in
Warsaw 1946.

15. Issy with another survivor travelling to England on the
Swedish Red Cross ship Ragne.

16. Rabbi Dr Solomon Schonfeld, with whom in 1946 Issy travelled to England on the Swedish Red Cross ship, arriving at Tower Bridge, London.

17. Issy's Aunt Gittla, his mother's sister, London 1939.

18. The Kazimierz Forest, where the SS executed hundreds of men, women and children.

19. Mass grave of Jews murdered by the Nazis in 1942 at Wilkuf (near Konin), site of a Polish Christian cemetery.

20. The author at one of the five graves in Kazimierz forest,
site of mass execution of Jews
(photograph by Theo Richmond).

14

21. Mushrooms growing in the Kazimierz Forest. Polish girls found gold rings and other jewellery on top of mushrooms as they pushed out of the ground.

22. Catholic icons inside Issy's Aunt Golda's friend's house when he visited her in 1987 on his return to Konin.

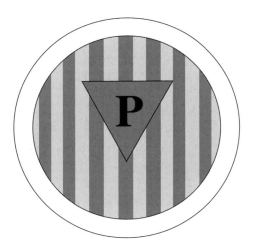

23. Symbol of his experience, designed by Issy.
The circle represents enclosure and loss of freedom;
the stripes represent camp uniforms and
the triangle with the letter P represents either
Political or Polish Prisoner.

ten per cent. We were hungry and demoralized but we still wanted to live. We had not given up hope.

On the way to the factory we had to pass the SS barracks. We would sometimes find potato peelings on the ground and take them back to our barracks to cook. The Germans had cans, corned beef for example, that held about a kilo. We took these empty cans because they were handy for soup or tea. If there was an extra can we would use it to cook in. We would sneak to the wires behind the barracks and cook anything we could find, which was mostly the potato peelings and leaves that blew in from nearby orchards. If one prisoner didn't have anything, another one did and we shared anything we managed to find between us. A prisoner on day shift would bring back the potato peelings and with all the SS there were loads of them. Of course, the Germans had to feed us a little bit too. The soup was thicker at this camp than anywhere else I had been and the rations of black bread a little bigger. As workers they thought we were useful to them.

The Mongolians in our barracks would bring back leaves they had collected in the mountains and put them under their bunks to dry out. If they found a piece of paper they would make a funnel and fill it with the dried leaves. If there was no paper, which was usually the case, they would take a leaf, stuff it with the dried leaves, tuck in the top and smoke it. Sometimes they were lucky enough to find a box of matches, perhaps given by an officer one of them might have worked for. They would find a bit of tin, sharpen it on the bricks until it was sharp enough to split through the matches and out of one match they would make four. Then they could have a smoke. It wasn't very pleasant and they would stink the barracks out with the smell of these leaves, which, I think, were cherry or apple. It was a disgusting smell.

One day after we'd finished our eight hours in the tank factory we were marching back to the camp when we noticed an underground shelter close to the SS barracks. From previous experience, and from the aroma coming from the ground, we knew this was the potato storage area. Some of the prisoners began grabbing potatoes and put them in the tin cups they carried. One prisoner got greedy and started stuffing potatoes inside his jacket. Of course the guard caught him and pulled him from the line. He made the prisoner give up all the potatoes and he was marched back to the camp.

Jakob the *Kapo* was sent for. Jakob was an extremely large man and was always called on to give the prisoners their punishment. The Germans assumed from his size that he was mean and would inflict the punishments they wanted. The guard must have told Jakob to give the potato thief 50 lashes – this was the normal punishment. Jakob had his own little office, a garden shed with a chair. The prisoner was taken inside for his lashing. Only when they got inside did Jakob say to the prisoner: 'You shout and scream and I'm going to hit the chair. I'm going to give you 50 lashes.' Every time the chair was struck the prisoner would give out a scream loud enough for everyone outside to hear. Jakob then told him: 'Put on your shirt. When you walk out of here I want you to walk like you've been badly hurt from the lashes I was supposed to inflict on you. Even if one prisoner sees you, you must show that you've been hurt. Keep on walking back to your barracks until you're out of sight of everyone.' The prisoner walked out holding his backside, limping badly.

One day the SS officers had Jakob put on a show for us. They built a wooden stage in the camp square with chairs all around for the officers. Jakob was called upon to perform extraordinary feats of strength for the amusement of the Germans. A small truck-load of stones was wheeled in for him to lift. No ordinary man could have lifted the stones – not even six men could have lifted them. Then he was given pieces of iron, which he dutifully bent into various shapes, all to the great satisfaction of the camp hierarchy. The Germans admired a person of strength such as Jakob. He was lucky they didn't do anything else to him.

Not a word about Jakob's phony beatings was said. Jakob was also frightened in case someone told the SS he wasn't doing his job properly. For a piece of bread, or half a loaf of bread, or a quarter of a loaf of bread, or a cigarette, you could buy information from anybody in the camp. Hunger would turn anyone into an informer. There was nothing you could do, it was just a way of life.

I saw this in other camps as well. Many people informed for

food. Some thought it would save their lives if they informed on other prisoners, but it wasn't true. If there were any mass executions, cremations, any transport that arrived, it didn't make any difference to the Germans. If they didn't want you to live, you didn't live. You were put on to transports made up of people they had no use for. They didn't want to save any of our lives anyway. The only prisoners they would leave alone were the ones they could make use of. I was a young boy and strong enough. But then, how much could we do? We had to pick up scraps of food like pigs, a bit here, a bit there. How much work can a person do when he's hungry? Besides, by now we were more than hungry, we were demoralized. But we still couldn't give up hope that our day would come.

One morning we were dragging ourselves off our bunks to go to work, when I found I couldn't lift my head. My body felt very hot and all I wanted to do was sleep. We had to hurry when we were called, but on this day I couldn't move. Karol, who always slept next to me, said: 'What's the matter, are you coming?'

'I can't', I whispered, 'I can't move my head, I feel terrible, I feel like my body's burning.' I was licking my lips, they were so dry, but there was nothing I could do. 'You go. If they ask why they are one short, say I couldn't go, say I'm lying on the bunk', I told him. Karol looked at me; he had tears in his eyes, he thought something was terribly wrong. I didn't want to discourage him but I did feel terribly ill. 'You go', I said, 'and report it to the *Stubenälteste*' (the foreman, or manager of the barrack). Our *Stubenälteste* was a German prisoner who had committed murder before the war; they had moved him from the ordinary prison to Leitmeritz and made him manager over our barracks. He could be vicious but no one was really frightened of him.

I lay in my bunk for a good hour or so after Karol left, not even able to lift my head off the mattress, when four prisoners in striped suits with white armbands bearing the word *Krankenstelle* arrived with a stretcher and took me down from my third tier. Handing me to one another carefully, they laid me on the stretcher. After about five minutes we came to the end of the camp and went through a gate I didn't even know existed. There was a big white signpost in the ground bearing a skull and cross-bones and the words 'No Entry – Typhus'.

The hospital doctor, a Polish prisoner, was informed that I was suspected of having typhus and the stretcher-bearers were instructed where to lay me on the floor. All prisoners in the typhus barracks were stripped of their clothing and laid on straw mattresses on the floor, like animals in a barn. They said we weren't clean if we wore our uniforms and they thought it would reduce our temperatures if we were naked.

When the doctor arrived the next day, he was wearing his prison uniform and an armband which read 'Doctor'. There were two types of typhus; both could last up to six weeks. With one type, stomach typhus, you would have severe stomach pains. It used to drive some of the victims mad because there was no medication for it; whoever was strong got over it while the weaker ones just died on the straw. I was fortunate because I had what they called 'blemish typhus', which left red blotches on your skin. In some cases it can remain for ever.

I lay on the straw, burning with fever, unable to move, my mind in a jumble. I thought my number was up. But the one thought that kept recurring was: 'What will Karol do? Who will look after him? At least if we're together we can help one another.' I lay with tears in my eyes wondering where he was and why he hadn't come to find out about me. I just lay there naked on the straw mat. When the doctor opened the windows for air I saw prisoners working outside at the back of the barracks planting a garden. I talked to some of them, asking them to find out about Karol. I begged them to find out if he was still alive. When they returned one of them said to me: 'No one has seen him or heard of him.'

I could feel the tears flowing down my cheeks. What had happened to him? Had they killed him? Had he been sent somewhere else? I was depressed and very worried.

I enquired about Karol every day but there was no trace of him. Every day I had to tell myself not to give up: 'I've got to stay alive. Something will happen. It could be today, tomorrow, in a month, six months, but I must stay alive. I've endured so much throughout the years in camps, I'm entitled to survive. Why should I die now?'

No one could help. I had to help myself, which was not easy because there was no medication. I couldn't get anything, not even a drop of cold water when I wanted it, it was rationed. They gave us black tea and a slice of bread; some people couldn't even manage that, they were so weak. At least I was getting a little better because I could get to the window for fresh air.

Lying next to me was a Russian air force captain who had been shot down over Dresden and brought to Leitmeritz as a prisoner-of-war. The man's fever was so bad that he was hallucinating. He said his mother had sent him a letter and he had to collect it. He would climb on to the window ledge, put his hand out of the window and feel along the guttering looking for his letter. I was ill, but he was worse and I felt sorry for him.

Then the day came. We were getting our ration of food and I watched him try to push the bread into his mouth but he couldn't swallow. The fighter pilot once dressed with all the dignity of a Russian air force officer deserved a better ending. He took the bread and stretched his hand out, offering me his portion. His hand dropped with the bread still in it offering it to me with his fingers. He closed his hand and died. I cried because he didn't deserve to die such an undignified death. He died not as a heroic fighter pilot, but naked on a straw mat from this terrible disease, typhus. 'Why a man like him?' I kept thinking. 'Perhaps I'm next.' At the back of my mind what haunted me most was 'Where is my brother?'

One morning as I was getting better I was told it was time for me to move out of the typhus barracks. I could walk by now, so I dressed and put on my clogs. I walked slowly, with the help of two prisoners, to the main hospital building. It looked like an aeroplane hangar made into a hospital; there were prisoners on three-tier bunk beds all the way around the building, probably 80 or 90 men in all.

A plump Russian man with a shaven head ran about looking after all the prisoners. He was wearing a black suit with a square cut out of the back; sewn in its place was a piece of the standard striped uniform. His armband bore the words 'Chief Doctor'. 'You come over here, you've got a bunk down here', he told me. I was so glad to be on a bunk; perhaps I was better and wouldn't die. Perhaps they wouldn't kill me; otherwise why would they give me a bunk when they could have left me on the straw?

The Russian doctor had been an officer and doctor with the Russian army before he arrived at Leitmeritz as a prisoner-of-war. He was a man in a million; he did whatever he could for each and every prisoner. He took temperatures but he had no medicine to give, only half a tin mug of water. He did whatever he could but his hands were tied; there was nothing he could give us. We had to get better through sheer determination; we had to will ourselves to become well again. Nevertheless, hundreds died daily from typhus.

Every day I felt a little better and began walking up and down talking to the other prisoners. One day I saw Karol lying on the top bunk at the other end of the hospital. I wept and so did he. At last we had found one another and we were both alive.

Karol had been taken ill with typhus two days after me and that was why the other prisoners couldn't find him: he was in the hospital too. It was like finding a million dollars. After all, we had never been parted; right through the war we had never been apart. If we had to pretend we weren't brothers, we weren't brothers, if we wanted to be brothers, we were brothers; but we never separated. We had to lie at times and say we were just friends even to other prisoners because we never knew how they might use such information. We could be sold for a cigarette or a slice of bread if anybody could get hold of it, so we kept to ourselves.

It was another four weeks before I went back to the regular barracks. One night as we lay in our bunks I could hear thunder – it seemed an unusual time of the year for thunder. A rumour started that it must be artillery fire. Now it is obvious, but then we didn't realize what was about to take place.

16 · Death Train to Landeshut

The next day all the prisoners were made to assemble in the camp square. Even though we were already separated according to nationality the SS now wanted us completely segregated. They wanted all the younger prisoners to form one group. I was in this group because I was 17. The oldest of the younger prisoners was 16 or 17, but by now we had the same experience as the older prisoners – being shifted from camp to camp, train to train, place to place. I had to be as wise as a man of 60, or I would have been dead by then.

After we were separated the SS and *Kapos* segregated us yet again. This time I could hear 'Jews on this side, Poles this side, Russians this side'. They continued until all the nationalities had been called. Most of the younger prisoners were Jewish, including Karol and myself. I knew what was coming, I had seen it before. Karol and I moved to the side with the other Polish boys and passed ourselves off as gentiles. I didn't want to go with the Jewish boys. I still don't know to this day what happened to those young boys. Then we were all taken out of the camp, 200 of us at most.

The SS had gathered us all together but I don't think they knew what to do with us. They didn't want us to be captured by the Russians because they knew that if we were, they themselves would be transported to Russia. It was possible that they could be held there for years before they were released, if they survived. In some camps the Germans just left the prisoners unguarded in a last-minute effort to save their own lives. We weren't so lucky.

We marched out of the camp across the fields to waiting trains, just as when we first arrived at the camp. This time, however, there was one engine facing in one direction and another engine facing the other. Of course we didn't know which way was east, west, north or south. We were taken to the train with four open wagons and a small engine. Because we were young we got to ride in the open wagons.

We pushed and shoved one another to get on the train because we had been told to get on quickly. If you didn't move quickly enough you would be hit with a rifle butt. Shoulders, back, head – they didn't care where they hit you as long as you got on the train as quickly as possible. Eventually all the prisoners were on the train. As the door closed behind us we could hear the other prisoners being herded on to the train going in the opposite direction. There wasn't enough room for all the prisoners so we had to wait for more trains.

It began to snow. We scrambled to the corners of the wagon to get away from the wind and snow blowing over the open top. We sat on the floor, huddling together, hoping we would be alright. Night was falling and the sky was growing darker and darker but the train still had not moved.

It was so quiet. You could hear only the hum of the engine. We sat in the darkness wondering where they were going to take us. I only had one thought in mind: perhaps they were taking us to the gas chambers. Perhaps we would be better off there. What we had been through in the last months was unbearable and indescribable. We were not treated as humans, we were treated worse than animals, with not the slightest element of compassion.

Some time in the middle of the night I felt the train give a jerk and I could hear the puffing of the engine. We started to move. I could smell the smoke from the engine and see the sparks from the wheels as we gathered speed. We travelled through the night into day, then night again, then daylight once more. This was all we knew of time – night and day. We couldn't even tell the difference between early morning and afternoon.

Suddenly the train stopped and the guards got out of the last wagon, a passenger wagon enclosed against the cold. Our wagon doors were opened; we were in the middle of nowhere. Then the shouting began: '*Achtung! Achtung!*' We jumped off the train leaving behind those who didn't have the strength to move.

There was snow everywhere. We grappled for handfuls of

snow; we hadn't eaten anything in two days. We made snowballs and threw them to the prisoners on the train. After about 15 minutes we were ordered back on the train; it was around half an hour before we moved again. Red Cross trains passed us going in the opposite direction. Of course we didn't know where they were headed because we didn't know where we were. But at least the SS guards weren't on our backs; we were happy about that.

The train carried on at a steady speed, in no hurry at all, into the third night. Suddenly we stopped again. It was very quiet. I thought everyone must have fallen asleep. Then the rumbling began again. We thought it was artillery fire, and prayed that the front line was getting nearer. 'Perhaps we're going to be liberated', I thought. 'Perhaps a miracle will happen.' Perhaps I was dreaming.

But we had to wait. Even with all of this going on, the Germans weren't in too much of a hurry to get rid of us. We had to wait until the guards got some kind of order stating what they should do with us. They couldn't make this kind of decision for themselves; they had to wait for a phone call or a message from higher authorities.

The next day we carried on with the journey, surviving on snow. After a few more days we stopped again. After a while, we heard the sound of a train approaching. When the train passed, travelling in the opposite direction, I could see it was full of soldiers and artillery. About 30 minutes later another train passed carrying a similar cargo. Then another and another. We knew something was going on but we weren't sure what. There was some sort of mass evacuation from somewhere. It looked like the army was moving back. Everything we saw on the passing trains gave the impression they were coming from a battle field and it was obvious these soldiers hadn't been sitting around guarding a camp somewhere. The SS guarding us must have thought themselves damned lucky they weren't on the other trains.

As we sat idle on the train, the puffing of the engine died out, the sky became darker and darker and the air grew colder and colder. We thought the driver must have gone to sleep because it was so quiet. We sat close together, huddling together to keep warm. Those prisoners who couldn't take the punishment any longer died from the freezing cold – youngsters, cold and hungry in an open cattle truck in the middle of nowhere. It was now around December 1944–January 1945.

17 · Landeshut Camp

Around daylight we could hear cars approaching. Two Mercedes Benz convertibles pulled alongside the train on roads cleared by army trucks. The SS officers got off the train to greet the visitors. *'Heil Hitler!'* Over and over again we heard this greeting.

The guards opened the wagon doors. As we got off the trains we were ordered to group into threes, just as we had learned to do from the beginning of our imprisonment. We were glad to get off the train at last, even though we didn't know what would happen to us next.

The two cars left and we were ordered to march. Eventually, we came to a mountain range. Just beyond a hill we could see another camp below us. We felt a sense of relief. No matter how badly we felt or how badly off and hungry we were, we could hear the prisoners mumbling: 'We're back home. Thank God we're back home.' At least we knew we could be warm again and perhaps have a bit of food. We marched down the hill – it was easier going down – and through the camp gates of Landeshut. We weren't far from Salzburg, across the River Danube from Leitmeritz.

In the camp square we went through the normal routine. We were formed into threes and given a set of orders: 'Attention!', 'Rest!', 'Hats off!' An SS officer came with a clipboard to take our numbers and we were dismissed. There was only one barracks in this camp and it was like no other camp I had been in. It was a two-storey brick building housing about 800 prisoners. The warmth of the barracks hit us as we went inside and we thought we were in heaven.

There were about 500 prisoners in the camp before we arrived, all Polish political prisoners who had taken part in the Warsaw uprising. They were brought especially to the camp and were lucky to be alive. The camp was surrounded by ordinary barbed wire instead of electrical wire. The Germans must have thought no one would try to escape: you would never be able to find your way out of the mountains. The other prisoners told us we were in Czechoslovakia. We couldn't believe it. Wherever it was, it was better than being on a train going nowhere.

There was one particular boy in this camp, a Ukrainian boy whose face I couldn't forget, who used to stand by the washroom smoking cigarettes made out of dry weeds. He was always smoking; he didn't know what to smoke, you could give him anything and he would just light it and put it in his mouth.

One day inside the washroom he said to me: 'I know you're a Jew.'

'Am I?', I said, 'I'm as much a Jew as you are.' He didn't answer, we left the washroom and that was the end of our conversation. But I didn't trust him.

I called on one of the Warsaw uprising prisoners, a man known as 'the leader'. I said to him: 'I'm going to put my life in your hands, and also my brother's, who is here with me. We go under different names. In other camps, if anybody was related to another prisoner they would be separated most of the time so we always went under different names. But we're Jewish. Now it's up to you what you do with us, but I'd rather trust you than the German SS or this Ukrainian boy who said I was Jewish. I think he was threatening to inform the SS that my brother and I are Jewish. He doesn't know for sure: I probably look more like a non-Jew than he does. But I don't trust him.'

The 'leader' said to me: 'Don't worry about it. You just carry on as normal. He won't say anything. Because if he does I know what to do with him.' The man knew we were the only two Jewish boys in the camp.

A little later I saw three or four men walk into the washroom with the Ukrainian boy and lock the door behind them. I didn't know what they said until afterwards when the 'leader' called me aside and told me what happened: 'He will be watched. You keep on watching him too. If he says one wrong word he will be strangled during the night. He won't live until morning.'

'Thank you very much', I said. 'If the Germans haven't killed me up to now I don't want a boy like that to inform on me.'

The boy kept out of my way for a few days and then tried to get friendly with me. He didn't say a lot but he had a cigarette – not that it was a real cigarette, it was leaves and God knows what – and he asked me if I wanted a puff. I said: 'No, I don't smoke.' He wouldn't leave me alone. He was trying to be too friendly, but at least I could keep an eye on him. The closer he was, the more I could watch him.

One day Karol and I went to the washroom and found the Ukrainian boy alone, smoking as usual. He was a little bit older then me, maybe 17, but had no sense at all. I hated him for what he'd said to me because he couldn't know for sure if he was right. 'Now listen to me', I warned, 'perhaps we'll all survive this camp. If we survive, you had better run before we do because if you don't, you'll be dead for what you said to me.' He didn't answer.

The 'leader' walked in to wash his hands and the boy and Karol walked out. He said to me: 'What you told me about this boy doesn't make any difference. We know all about him. If anything happens he's going to be dead anyway. He informed on a lot of people in the camp before this, before you were here.'

'Oh', I said, 'he's a professional informer! I've seen it before in other camps. People would sell their soul for a piece of bread. He's one of them. It's good to know.'

We didn't do much of anything at Landeshut, just lazed about. The barracks was like a big hotel or convalescent home with heating pipes that ran along the walls. We would go to the square or the washroom and look out of the windows – from upstairs you could see the whole camp – or we would go to the wires and watch the German guards busy with the trucks and cars. Officers were always coming and going. I guess it was like a safe haven to them, right in the middle of the mountains. It must have been a godsend to the guards because they didn't have much to do either.

We were fed twice a day on soup with bits of cabbage in it and sometimes beans and bread. Whatever it happened to be, it was left over from the guards' kitchen and it kept us going. I don't think the SS got such good food either because we were in the mountains where they couldn't get regular supplies.

There was an inspection three times a day. We would line up in threes while three or four guards and an officer with a clipboard would look at the numbers on our arms, write them down and dismiss us. It was the same every day: on parade, counted, and dismissed. We spent a lot of time in the barracks as it was warm inside and we could come and go as we pleased. Some of the prisoners even invented games to play inside.

I had seen no killing in the camp, which was a very positive sign. Perhaps we would survive. Every day there were hopes of being set free. We knew spring was approaching because every day on parade it was getting warmer and warmer; the sun was coming out and we felt a little happier.

The word around the camp was that General Sikorski, who was with the Polish government-in-exile in London, had died in an aircrash. We heard the pilot survived, but the general and his daughter were lost. Some of the prisoners thought this meant that Poland now had no chance of surviving the war.

The fighters from Warsaw had good memories for dates and times and had kept track of the days since their arrival. It was now April 1945. It was a nice warm morning and I could smell the grass from the mountains. We were standing outside being counted as usual and I watched the birds flying, thinking: 'Look at these birds, at least they are free, they can go wherever they want. We can't. Maybe one day.'

It was 9 May 1945, about five o'clock in the morning; we had had our last roll call the previous day. We went to the first floor of our barracks and watched the SS running around in confusion. Suddenly six trucks drove up and the SS started loading the trucks with everything they had, bedding and other items. The whole camp grew restless.

That night no one could sleep. It was as if we had had a forewarning that something was about to happen. No one slept all night; we lay awake whispering in the dark. A couple of prisoners stood by the door in case anyone walked up.

About four o'clock in the morning we noticed a few

prisoners were missing – the Ukrainian boy and six others. Just as it was getting light we heard shots fired. When we looked out there were seven bodies wedged between the fence wires. They had tried to escape.

The Ukrainian boy never told anyone about Karol and me being Jewish. Though I threatened him, I never really wished him dead. I never thought he was foolish enough to try to cross the wires, but maybe his patience ran out, or maybe he noticed something. A lot of trucks and guards had left the camp. If they thought the Germans were gone, why didn't they go through the front gate instead of the wires? If only they'd waited a little longer.

18 · Liberation

A couple of hours later we heard artillery shelling again. We could see the shells landing on the mountains. We knew who it was. Nearer to six o'clock we heard tank chains squeaking and rattling into the camp. The tanks came down the hills and flattened the entire barbed-wire fence around the perimeter of the camp. They stopped, but no one got out. The advancing Russian army came in after the tanks and the shouting began.

'We're liberated! We're free!' There was much hugging and kissing of the soldiers who had snatched us back from hell to the world of the living.

Of course the first thing we did was run to the kitchen. Karol and I did manage to get some bread but we were too late for the soup. Some prisoners were on top of the soup drums. I saw a man standing with one foot in the soup kettle.

Having no luck in the kitchen, Karol and I went to the SS barracks. The SS had left everything behind to flee and evade capture: unfinished food and even guns lay on the tables. We were checking all around when Karol called to me: 'I was pushing this door to open it but someone's on the other side pushing it back and I can't get in.'

'I'll come with you', I said. 'You push the door open and I'll go behind the window.' I picked up an abandoned machine gun and stuck it through the opening of a narrow glass window panel. I looked behind and saw one guard standing in a corner and another behind the door pushing it closed as Karol tried to push it open. One was trying to put on a jacket and the other had a pair of trousers halfway over his uniform. I shouted at them in German: 'Put your hands up!' They stood with their hands up and I went around to the door and shouted: '*Raus! Raus! Raus!*'

'Don't shoot', one of them begged, 'We are Russians.'

'You are Russian? What are you doing in the SS guard

uniform, you pig!' I marched him to the camp square to a Russian officer who had emerged from one of the tanks. The Russian had many stars on his epaulettes so I knew he was a high-ranking officer. I told him I thought these were the two who had shot at the prisoners earlier that morning.

The officer looked at me and, completely out of the blue, said: 'Tell me, are there any Jews in this camp?'

I thought for a moment then answered: 'No, why do you ask?'

'I wanted to know.'

There was no one around except Karol, myself and the two SS guards so I took a chance and said to him in Yiddish: 'Are you Jewish yourself?'

'Yes, are there any other Jewish prisoners here?'

'Yes, us two', I said pointing to Karol and myself. To my amazement he spoke Yiddish very well. He had tears in his eyes: 'Have you been in other camps before this?'

'Yes, but this is the cleanest camp I have been to', he answered. 'I wouldn't like to tell you what the others are like.'

'You don't have to tell me, I know. I was there before you. Now look, I want to execute these two SS guards, I want revenge for what they have done and all the murders they have committed.'

'Don't do that', he said. 'Leave it to me.'

'Look at them. I feel I want to murder them like they murdered other people.'

'Don't worry about it. They won't live if I have my way. Let's go.'

He told another officer to search the guards. He made me stand beside him. The Russian officer noticed the new jackboots the SS guards were wearing and ordered them to take them off. As one of them took off the boots, his jacket sleeves rose up just enough for me to see three gold watches on one arm and two on the other.

'Take them off!', the Russian officer ordered. 'Give them to me!' When he examined the watches he saw on the back engravings of birthdays and anniversaries with Jewish names on them. He looked choked. 'Listen', I said, 'these watches belonged to people who are dead now. He probably murdered them himself.'

The Russian officer searched the SS guards again. He didn't find much at first, only tags sticking out from their collars. Finally one of the officers searched the front of the uniform, where the button holes were, and found something between the layers of material. He pulled out a medal, a black Iron Cross.

'You've done a good job', said the Russian. 'You've got a medal as well. This medal's for Danzig, isn't it?' Danzig is a Polish port and I didn't understand how they came to be in Czechoslovakia.

One of the Russians hit the SS man in the back: 'Come on you dogs, give them the jackboots. See these boys? They haven't worn a pair of leather boots since 1939 probably. Let them wear your boots, they're brand new.' I took a pair and gave Karol the other pair. We took off our clogs and put on the boots. They were a bit too big but we took them anyway.

The Russians led the two SS men out of the camp and I can only guess that they were executed. Which I was glad of because God alone knows how many people they had executed. They might have killed five whole families to get those five watches.

I went back to the tank and thanked the Russian officer. 'Now my brother and I will try to get back to Poland, to my town of Konin, and see if we can find any relatives who have survived these last five years.'

The Russian officer looked at me with tears in his eyes: 'Don't worry, lads. Perhaps you'll be lucky when you get back and find someone. I hope you do find your family alive.' He shook my hand and wished us well with all his heart.

19 · *Walking Back to Poland*

Karol and I walked out of the camp as quickly as possible. We passed through fields and woods and mountains, as far as we could, to get away from Landeshut. We saw smoke billowing in the distant sky; where it was coming from we didn't know.

After a while we reached a village and knocked at the first house we came to. A cleanly dressed German man in a suit, collar and tie answered the door: 'What do you want?', he asked us. When he saw our striped prison suits he stood still for a minute uncertain of our intentions.

'Have you got anything to eat?', I asked.

'One moment.' We stood by the door waiting while the old man went into a shed and brought out a shoe box. In eager anticipation I looked inside the box only to be disappointed, if not offended, by the offering. 'Perhaps you would like to eat that', I said, throwing the box filled with potatoes aside. 'We've had enough of these things for five years, it's your turn now.' Karol and I walked straight into the man's house, helping ourselves to freshly baked wholemeal bread lying on the table. '*Danke schön*', I said sarcastically as we walked out clinging on to the bread as if it were gold.

We stayed on the main road that led out of town and came upon a train sitting on tracks at the edge of a forest. Smoke was billowing out of the engine of the train, which was waiting to continue its journey. We happened to spot an old wooden shed close by and decided it was time to take a rest. Karol followed me around to the back of the shed and to our surprise we discovered four Russian soldiers and an officer hiding there. Another five soldiers had set up a small artillery camp close by. One of them called out to us: 'Come over here, comrades. I see you've come out of the concentration camps.' They seemed to show us a lot of respect. 'Do you see this train over there?', they asked. 'Lie down on this bank and you'll see what's going to happen.'

As the train moved, the Russians fired. The shells landed on the tracks in front of the train. One of the shells smashed into the engine; smoke blew out with intense pressure. An officer turned to me. 'Have a look', he said and he handed me his binoculars. The German guards were jumping off the train in all directions, running for their lives into the forest. There were explosions everywhere as the shells blew the train into smithereens.

'Watch this!', said the Russian. They loaded their guns again; two were handed the shells by a third man. One man opened the chamber of his gun while the other loaded it. Each time they loaded the gun they increased the distance of the shot. The train was finally blown into non-existence. We were caught up in the front line between the Germans and the Russians.

Karol and I decided to keep moving in the direction of home and the Russian soldiers wished us well as we started off again. We were hoping to reach a motorway to help us find our bearings but we didn't even know which direction to walk in.

After a few miles we stopped to have a piece of bread and a rest. We could hear horses and carts in the distance. Finally we saw a column of German evacuees going in the opposite direction; they were moving their entire houses – bedding, wardrobes, furniture, tables, chairs, everything. I think there must have been about 30 wagons. We stopped them and asked if they had anything to eat. One man went to his wagon and got a piece of bread and a small pat of butter for us.

As we stood enjoying the gift we heard gun shots. Across the field were Russian soldiers holding their machine guns with one hand, shooting them into the air. The Germans became frightened and everyone went very quiet.

The Russians saw Karol and me in our prison clothes and called to us: 'Comrades! You're from the concentration camps. Do you speak German?'

'Yes, I do', I answered.

'Good, I'll give you my hat and you ask them if they have any gold. I want it all put in the hat.'

Karol and I were given forage caps and we walked to each wagon announcing in German: 'If you've got any gold you'd better give it up or they'll shoot you.' Whatever they had, rings or anything, they took off and put in the caps. The

Russians went through the caps, put the gold into their breast pockets, and ran back towards the forest.

Karol and I kept walking, not knowing where we were, until we came to a farmhouse. We expected to see someone or hear a shout or even see a dog, but there was nothing. The farmhouse was abandoned. I guess the owners must have been afraid of the shelling and left. In the kitchen we found stale bread and butter in the dishes. Nothing had been touched. We helped ourselves, slowly because we had been told by a Russian doctor in one of the camps that we shouldn't eat a lot of fat after not having eaten properly for so long.

We had a restless night in the strange house and the next day we decided to continue our journey. Perhaps someone from our family was waiting at home in Konin for our return. On through the fields we went. I didn't want to walk along the main roads and run the risk of meeting the Russians again: God knows what tricks they would be up to. However, we were not frightened of any of our Russian liberators – they showed respect for our camp uniform.

Finally we came to the *autobahn*, Hitler's prestigious motorway. There were hundreds, maybe thousands, of people walking along the motorway coming from every direction. There were prisoners-of-war – Russians, Poles, even English ones – walking towards Poland. They were heading in that direction because everything in Germany was flattened, whereas Poland still had some transport that functioned. Moving in the opposite direction, towards Berlin, were heavy American trucks and Russian soldiers with artillery guns and something I'd never seen before: Polish soldiers with heavy artillery weapons. They were the front-line support divisions.

From a distance we saw hundreds of people gathered in a field, like swarms of bees. No one was moving, they were all standing in a circle. Perhaps we could get transport here, I thought, because there were a great many trucks on the motorway.

In the middle of the circle, surrounded by jeeps, there were wide tables formed in the shape of a horseshoe. Behind the tables were high-ranking Russian officers with clipboards and thick books. The Russian guards had red bands on their arms with the letters NKVD – the Soviet secret police, or Russian security services.

Everybody had to form into a line and pass in front of the tables. Each person was asked for some sort of identification to prove who they were and where they came from. Of course, we had nothing except our black and white striped prison clothes, but we did have something that intrigued the Russian officers. We pulled up our sleeves to show the numbers tattooed on our arms. The Russians mumbled to one another. I think we were the first two young prisoners they had come across with these tattoos. They were glad to see people like us and other prisoners-of-war who had survived and they honoured us by giving us preference to move on.

The ex-soldiers of any nationality were put to one side and given transport wherever they wanted to go. Most of them wanted to reach a port where they could get a ship to their home countries. Some even asked where they could get an aeroplane and were told to go to the American or English delegates, who were mostly based in Germany. The soldiers they were mainly looking for were the Ukrainians. There were about four or five Ukrainians just behind us in the queue and I heard a Russian officer ask one of them: 'Where's your documentation?' The Ukrainian took out the passport given to him by the Germans bearing insignia of an eagle and swastika on the front.

'How is it that you are a Ukrainian but have a German passport?'

'I was taken to work – forced labour', answered the Ukrainian.

'That's not true. You didn't have to go if you didn't want to. You volunteered. You went to fight with the Germans against us. I have a job for people like you.' He tore up the passport and those of the other Ukrainians and took them across the road to the NKVD. They filled up the trucks with Ukrainians and took them away towards Berlin. One Russian said to me: 'We have plenty of work for them. They can clean up the bombsites. If they can work for Germany, they can work for us.' I had a smile on my face: I had experienced the brutal behaviour of some of these Ukrainians as guards in the concentration camps.

20 · With the Red Cross

Karol and I made our way along the *autobahn*, in the direction the Russians had told us, towards Poland. We crossed a field and came to the River Oder. I had learned in school that this river ran along the border between Germany and Poland. The boundaries, of course, had changed since the advent of the Third Reich. If we could find a place in the river narrow enough to cross we would be nearly into Poland.

The Oder is a wide river and we were lucky the tide was out when we found a crossing point, otherwise we would have lost a day's journey. We followed the river for about four miles until we came to a flat place where we could see the sand on the river bed. We continued across the fields on the other side of the river.

There were buildings in the distance and I thought perhaps it was a Polish city. I guess we hadn't travelled as far as I had imagined because it turned out to be the city of Breslau. Walking into Breslau, we saw some of the houses were razed to the ground and many of the the taller buildings had lost their top floors.

The buildings had been demolished by Katyusha artillery guns. These rocket launchers could shoot 320 shells in 25 seconds. They had to be transported on the back of large trucks. The trucks were fitted with mines so that if there was a danger of being captured the soldiers would blow up the guns and the Germans would never obtain the secret of the Katyusha. In my opinion, these guns won the war for the Russians.

As we walked through the city we saw no one; it was a ghost town. On the outskirts of the town we were intrigued by a large and obviously new cemetery. It was very tidy and filled with graves, dotted by markers bearing crosses and the names of Russian soldiers. The cemetery was guarded by an iron gate supported by vast pillars on either side. Majestically placed on top of the pillars were Russian army tanks. In the middle of the cemetery was another tank which bore the name of a Russian general. It was written in old Russian lettering and we couldn't make it out.

As I looked at the hundreds of graves I said to Karol: 'Look at all these people, all these young innocent boys who died.' I felt for them because I had seen many Russian soldiers killed. We had seen cemeteries for German soldiers too but they tended to be neglected.

Eventually we left Breslau and walked on through various villages until we got to Poland. I knew we were in Poland by the style of the houses we passed. We went to a little house with a thatched roof and knocked on the door. An old man answered from inside: 'What do you want?' He stopped still when he came to the door and saw us.

'Could you give us some water to drink?', we asked.

'Come in. Sit here on the bench. I'll give you better than water, have some coffee.' He poured the coffee into big tin mugs and passed it to us. 'Sugar I haven't got, you'll have to take it as it is', he apologized.

'Don't worry about it!', Karol said.

'Do you want any bread with it?', the man asked.

'We don't want to take your bread unless you have some to spare.'

'I've got spare, our neighbours always bake for one another', he insisted.

Karol and I ate the bread and drank the coffee and felt much better. 'Where are we?', I asked the man.

'In another 15 miles or so you'll be in Katowice. It's a large city in Poland and very nice. They have electric trams running in the streets', he bragged.

It was June and the weather was warm. In the city we followed the tram lines until we came to a corner building with a Red Cross flag hanging from the side. We took our time walking, looking at the lovely city. There was an occasional demolished house, but not many.

The aroma of simmering soup made my mouth water as we entered the Red Cross. 'Could we have some food?', I asked one of the men working there. There were a few men there but it was mostly women.

'Of course you can', he answered. 'Are you from a concentration camp?'

'Yes', I replied. 'It took us a few weeks to get here because we had no transport.'

Karol and I smiled at each other when we saw the large plates of soup and bread they gave us. The soup was filled with potatoes and cabbage and to us it was a five-star meal. We ate two portions each. When I asked if there was any place to stay, one of the men said: 'We've got some room upstairs, there are two floors. You can have any bed you like.'

'Can we stay here two or three days?', I asked.

'You can stay here a week or two if you like. That's what we're here for, to help.'

'Can I come down to eat something later? Will there be anything to eat?'

'Yes, in the evening', he said smiling.

Upstairs we found a big room with 12 beds. Now we had soft beds too. It was like staying in a hotel. On our fourth day at the Red Cross we decided to continue on to Konin.

When we got to the station there were hundreds of people waiting, but no trains in sight. Finally we heard a train approaching but as it neared the platform I could see hundreds of people stuck to it like flies, inside and out. The only place Karol and I could find to ride was on the flat roof.

We had to be careful not to fall off. It wasn't too bad, except for the smoke from the engine blowing in our faces. We lay down and covered our faces with our striped caps to keep the smoke out of our eyes. The train kept stopping for water and to load up with coal. About 24 hours passed until we pulled into Poznań. Konin was some 60 miles away.

We weren't sure where to find another train that would take us to Konin so we followed the crowds of people. After about two hours of waiting, hoping the next train that came along wouldn't be as full as the last one, a train arrived that was passing through Konin *en route* to Warsaw. This train too was packed solid; there wasn't even room to hang on anywhere. We pushed our way forward and managed to find a space in between two wagons. We sat on the buffers holding on to the handles by the steps. We were lucky to find this space. Other people might have been too frightened to ride this way, but we weren't. We would have done anything to reach our destination.

All we wanted was to get home. I was excited, yet frightened, wondering who would or would not return. I hoped against hope that someone in the family was still alive, waiting there to see who might return.

21 · Return to the Ghost Town of Konin

It was a couple of hours before we reached the familiar station in Konin. When Karol and I looked around, it was as if someone had stabbed us in the heart with a knife. I looked at him, he looked at me and we both had tears in our eyes. We never expected to return without our family.

We didn't know what to expect as we walked further into the town. It was very painful. Was anybody waiting for us? Perhaps we would see a familiar face that would give us a bit of hope. We were full of apprehension over what we might see. We were praying, in our own way, as we walked: 'Please! Perhaps someone will be there to see who's coming home!' We walked the two miles from the station to our house, hoping everything would be as we'd left it in 1939. Our thoughts were always the same: 'Perhaps there'll be a miracle.'

Konin's main street was deserted. The old clock on top of the town hall was still there, ringing every quarter of the hour just as it always had. Every evening before the war you would see most of the town in Market Square: men, women, boys with their girlfriends. It had been a lively place, with cars and trams passing through the brightly lit square. But not now. There had been lots of shops on both sides of the street, but not now. The shops had been turned into accommodation for Polish families, the front doors shut tight as if the inhabitants were frightened to come out into the day. We were living in a different world now. We were living under Russian communism. It was a very unhappy life, full of restrictions.

Standing at the corner of Castle Square, I saw the synagogue I had been so used to seeing every day for the first 13 years of my life. The closer we walked to the barren plot of land where our house should have been, the more tearful Karol and I became. Why wasn't the house there? Had it been bombed? Why had it been destroyed? There were five or six other houses on that corner that were demolished as well. All the corner houses next to the square had been knocked down to enlarge the square area. There was nothing left, only dirt.

At the other side of the square, about 100 yards down a small street, on the left, was the house that had belonged to my grandparents. People were still living on the ground floor where my grandparents had lived. Karol and I walked into the familiar house without saying a word to the new tenants. I walked down the corridor and upstairs to the two, now empty, rooms my aunt had lived in. I looked at Karol and said: 'Perhaps we'll stay here. We've nowhere else to go.' We were overwhelmed by an extraordinary pain which only the two of us could feel.

'We may as well try', said Karol, 'but we'll have to sleep on the floor.'

'Well, for one or two nights we might have to. We're used to it, anyway. Let's go and have a look around and we'll come back here tonight.'

We went out, closing the door behind us. The next day the people who were living downstairs moved out. I thought of taking the ground floor but I couldn't: I found the idea of moving into my grandparents' home too upsetting. 'We've got to get away from here', I told Karol, 'it brings back too many memories.'

Out in the town we met up with a few other Jewish people who had also returned from the camps. We recognized some of them from before the war. After five years we still knew each other. We were home now, but we still had to fend for ourselves.

There was no one else around the town, only Russian soldiers and intelligence people with trucks and jeeps and machine guns patrolling the area like the Germans had done. In the autumn of 1939 the streets had been full of German intelligence agents. These people came into the town wearing the latest civilian fashions and, in perfect Polish, started the rumours of the impending war. Even with the sort of panic they had created, there was no way of preparing for what actually occurred. The older generation had remembered the First World War and the German occupation at that time. The soldiers, my grandparents said, had been human beings, gentlemanly even, bringing food and supplies the people needed. More importantly, there had been no distinction between Jews and Christians then.

A Red Cross flag hung outside a familiar building. When we went through the open doors into a corridor that led into a main hall, we could smell food. We were given metal plates full of hot soup and black bread. These plates must have been left behind by the Germans because we didn't have anything like them in Poland before the war.

The hall was quite big, with several large tables. The back door was open to let in the warm summer breeze. Sitting there looking through the windows, I remembered the lake, formed by the water from the power station, where we canoed as children. Occasionally we went to the River Warta, but the canoes were home-made so we couldn't take any chances with the river's surges and currents. This small still lake was just fine. All we could see through the windows now were Russian trucks.

Sitting in the Red Cross building, everything began to come back to us. We fell asleep at the table for a couple of hours; we weren't in a hurry, we had nowhere to go. After our nap I asked the Red Cross man: 'Is there any chance we could get some different clothes? We can't walk around in these camp suits any more.'

'I tell you what', he said. 'Come back here tomorrow for dinner and we will see what we can sort out then.'

The Red Cross were having a hard time obtaining supplies. They had to get food donated from farmers nearby. And they didn't know what money to use: the Polish zloty was worthless now. During the German occupation the Polish currency was in operation here but nothing else, and you couldn't use it outside Poland. The Germans produced it for the Poles and it disappeared with the Germans. The main currency in Poland after the war was the dollar; everybody was looking for the American dollar. Not many people knew what a dollar looked like, much less possessed one. The only people who could possibly have had dollars were people who had relatives in the United States who sent them to their Polish families.

'Thank you very much', I said to the Red Cross man. We went back for meals for the next couple of days but no clothes appeared. On the third day I asked again.

'Someone promised me something for tomorrow', he told us. 'Come back in the morning just before dinner about 12 o'clock and we'll sort it out.' The next day the man stood behind the counter. 'Good, you're here', he said as we walked in.

'Have you got anything for us?'

'Yes, come with me.' We followed him into an office, behind the kitchen, to a laundry basket. 'Look, there's some stuff in there. See what you can salvage from this.' In the basket we discovered trousers and jackets, about eight sets in all. They were old Polish army uniforms, probably donated by demobbed soldiers. Karol and I tried on a jacket and found a couple that fitted well; they had great big pockets in front and we were pleased with them. We found trousers too but they were too long and we had to turn the bottoms up, and we needed belts.

'Is there anything we can have to hold our trousers up?'

'Well, I've got no belts. If you look you have loops around the waist on the trousers.'

'That's right, I've got to hold them around the loops probably just to keep them up.'

'No, I've got some string in this office you can have. Put that through the loops.' He cut some string and gave us each a piece to hold up our trousers.

'I feel a little bit more like myself now that I got out of those concentration-camp clothes and into civilian clothes', I said. 'I'm going to get rid of these other clothes myself.' We rolled up the striped uniforms except for the shirts, which we were still wearing.

We made our way back along the main street, through Market Square and across the bridge to the river where I swam as a little boy. It was a lovely hot day. Karol and I carried the parcels of concentration-camp clothes under our arms as we walked along a dusty back road to the river. This had been a place where people came to laze about in the sun, to swim and enjoy themselves before the war.

We took off our shirts, washed them in the river and hung them on bushes along the river's edge. We made ourselves comfortable on the sand waiting for the shirts to dry and fell asleep until evening. The shirts were warm and dry when we put them back on.

As we were walking away from the river we saw a man burning weeds. We asked him: 'Is it alright if we burn these clothes here?'

'Burn them? Where did you get them from?'

'Off my body!', I said.

'I don't believe you.'

'Yes, off my body! And these are my brother's, off his body!'

'How come?'

'Well, that's how it was', I said. And here's something to prove it.' I showed the man my tattooed number.

He put his hand on my shoulder. 'God bless you boys!' With that we slung the uniforms into the burning weeds and watched the smoke rise. The odour from the fire was very different from the odours at Auschwitz. I could now smell weeds and linen from the concentration-camp uniforms, instead of burning flesh. Once again I was reminded that it could have been me.

We walked away from the burning uniforms, down the dusty road and across the bridge into Market Square again. The emptiness of the square reminded me of 1939 when the Germans had imposed a curfew on the town and no one could go out after five o'clock.

Karol and I could see that we couldn't stay; there was no point. It was like before the war when the Germans took over. We could see the same things happening under communism. We had learned about Stalin in the camps and my grandfather used to tell me a lot of stories about the Russians from the First World War. Nothing we heard was as bad as it really was. We both knew the only reason we stayed in Konin was to give anyone in our family who had survived the chance to come home and find us there. It was a vain hope.

The man at the Red Cross asked us if we were happy with our clothes. 'They couldn't be any better', I said.

'I'll try to find a couple of shirts', he offered. 'Maybe tomorrow, I'll ask around to see if anyone has a couple of spare shirts in your size.'

A few more people came in to have something to eat,

maybe 20 or 30. So many people didn't have anything and had nowhere else to go, they had to rely on the Red Cross to keep them going. We usually got there when the place was empty and never saw this many people. Now we'd got rid of the camp uniforms, we were just a couple of Polish boys sitting there having something to eat. It didn't matter to us that our new clothes were of military style.

22 · Encounter with Collaborators

I decided to try and find Veronika Zabochinska, an old friend of the family. She had lived next door to us before the war with her husband, Kaźek, their two children and his widowed mother. Karol said he was going back to the house where we were staying and I told him I would see him there soon.

In the square I asked a woman: 'Do you know where Veronika Zabochinska lives? And Jadwiga Morowska?'

The woman stared through me: 'Do you know me?'

'No.'

'If I were you I wouldn't have anything to do with either of them', she warned.

'Why not?'

She pointed out the house where Veronika lived and then where Jadwiga Morowska lived. 'Good day', she said as she walked away.

I was anxious to visit Jadwiga Morowska so I went there first. When she answered the door I recognized her immediately. 'Do you know who I am?', I asked. She stared at me. 'What's the matter with you? Don't you know who I am? Have I changed so much? I am Srulek Hahn, your neighbour from six years ago. You knew me as a small boy.'

She knew who I was; she didn't want to have anything to do with me. Eventually she let me into her house and I sat in silence while she stood by the stove cooking. Suddenly I realized I was looking at my own mother's cooking utensils hanging on the wall around her stove. I walked out, slamming the door furiously. That was the last time I wanted to see Jadwiga Morowska.

Veronika Zabochinska lived on the first floor in a house across the square. I knocked on the door and an old lady with a scarf on her head stared out at me. I could tell she didn't recognize me.

Everyone stayed inside like prisoners behind closed doors. Not so much the younger ones, but the older people who grew up in Konin and had lived more or less normal lives under German occupation in the First World War. Now they would live happier lives under the Russians.

'Mrs Zabochinska, you don't recognize me. I am Mrs Hahn's oldest son.' She blushed. I wondered what was wrong with her. I stepped in and saw, on a big double bed in the next room, her daughter-in-law Veronika with her four children. When we had left six years ago she only had two children and now there were four. I couldn't work this out because her husband was killed when the war started in 1939. She didn't want to speak to me but I persevered.

'You probably don't remember', she began, 'but my husband, Każek, never returned from the war. Things were very hard. There was no work for me and my mother-in-law and I had to feed my two children. I had no food. I had no option so I found myself a German soldier for a boyfriend and I wasn't short of food. I had two children by him and we were supposed to get married but he was sent to the Russian front and I haven't heard from him. Now I am in serious trouble because the Polish secret police regard me as a traitor and they are going to deport us to East Germany.'

'You said I don't remember your husband, but I do. I remember when he worked as a builder. But why did you have to have a German for a boyfriend?'

'Under the circumstances I had no choice. I had no food.'

'That's why you have to pay for it now', I said.

I hadn't noticed anything belonging to my family in her house so I asked her about Jadwiga Morowska. 'I saw my mother's cooking utensils in her house and I was very upset to find them there.'

'Well, because you asked I will tell you. After your family was taken from your house by the Gestapo and deported...', she stopped short and looked at me, frightened to speak. I questioned her but she became emotional. Eventually she continued: 'I have nothing to lose now, I will tell you. Jadwiga Morowska and her daughter also had German boyfriends. Her daughter went to Germany with a friend; you remember Zosza Zabaczynska? They went to Germany as volunteer workers and never came back. Mrs Morowska is just as guilty as I am of having plenty of German boyfriends. But she's getting away with it because she had no children and she's a lot older than me. Not only that but she's carrying on with a Russian NKVD officer so nothing has happened to her yet. Three weeks after you were all deported, Jadwiga Morowska, with the help of some German soldiers, broke open the door of your house, took all your furniture and sold it. I suppose she kept all your mother's utensils. Be careful: don't have anything to do with her.'

23 · Imprisoned by Polish Security

At that moment there was a loud knock on the door. In walked two uniformed Polish secret police officers with pistols on their belts. They went straight for me: 'Who are you and what are you doing here?', they demanded.

'First of all, I know this woman and her mother-in-law, Mrs Zabochinska, from before the war', I replied. 'And what's more, lieutenant, I recognize you as well. But I'll tell you who I am. I am Ludwik Szwiatowicz's grandson. You also knew my uncles; we had the private car hire and taxi business. You were a barber and you used to cut their hair.' I remembered him standing by the door of the salon where he worked, combing his thick wavy blond hair as he watched the ladies walk by. I think he was embarrassed when I reminded him he used to be a barber. After all, he was now a second lieutenant in the Polish secret police.

'I have no choice but to arrest you. Let's go.' And I was escorted out of the house. I walked in between the two policemen. We turned a corner and came to a red brick building with two Polish flags hanging, slightly slanted, either side of the entrance. I knew exactly where I was. The building had an evil smell about it – it used to be the Gestapo headquarters.

The lieutenant reported to someone that we were there and, after a few minutes and no explanation, I was taken to one of the prison cells in the cellar. There were no beds in the cell, only wooden bunks with plenty of straw. The windows had bars and were level with the street. The door had a big circle with a bar through it for the guards to see through. There were guards 24 hours a day in the corridor with rifles hanging from their shoulders. Their behaviour reminded me of the Germans. I thought they were different but, once trained by the Russian secret service, they were no different at all.

Fourteen other men were in the cell, talking in tense whispers. One of them motioned to me: 'Here you are, boy, there's room for you here if you want. What are you in here for?'

'Do you know what you're in here for?', I returned the question.

'No.'

I thought perhaps I knew this man. 'Is your name Kśewicki?'

He looked at me puzzled. 'Who are you? How do you know me?'

'I remember when you were a caretaker before the war and you lived in the back of the house with the barber shop that belonged to Mr Kozłowski.' He hugged me and begged me to tell him who I was. 'Do you remember a family called Szwiatowicz?'

'Who, the owners of the taxis and the horses and carriages?'

'Yes, that was my grandfather.'

'Good God, I knew that grandfather of yours very well! What happened to him?'

'I'm afraid to tell you. He's no longer alive, or the family.' I could see the tears in his eyes.

'If we ever come out of this prison', he said, 'and you don't have anywhere to stay, come and stay with me.'

I thanked him. 'If I ever get out of here I would like to go abroad. I haven't any family here any more.'

I was in the prison for eight days without anyone telling me when or if I would be released. I was talking to my caretaker friend about the man who had arrested me. 'You know who he is; he worked for the barber Kozłowski where you lived and worked.'

'Yes, I still live there with my wife and daughter. I know who he is. He's Tadek the barber.'

'He turned out to be a fine bastard!', I muttered. 'I told him who I was and he arrested me, but without telling me why.'

'Have you seen all these men here? They've been here for two months without being told why.'

'I hope they don't keep me here for two months. I came out of the German concentration camps not long ago. I got rid of my German enemies but I can see that the Polish secret police are no different from the Gestapo.'

He whispered in my ear: 'I knew who he was and what he's done since. There are a few you know as well. A lot of boys went into the Polish secret service. He's a bastard. He's done a lot of harm to people. Don't worry, you'll come out of this alright.'

A face appeared at the cell door, spying on us. The guard watched us and I watched him. As his face disappeared something about him bothered me. The more he looked at us, the more bothered I became. I lay on the bunk racking my brains to figure out what bothered me about this guard, with his little red nose.

Suddenly it hit me. 'I know that guard!', I told my friend. 'Even dressed in a uniform, I know who he is! It's Juzek Kelducki!'

'The only Kelducki I know is a shoemaker', he said.

'Yes, that's his son. His father was a volunteer fireman. They were neighbours of my grandparents and I used to see him every day. I'm going to ask him if he remembers me.'

'You might get into more trouble', my friend warned.

'Don't worry', I assured him, 'after what I've been through, this doesn't worry me in the least.' I went to the door and in a soft voice called: 'Juzek, Juzek.' A face appeared in the spy hole. 'Juzek, do you remember me?'

'Jesus Christ, is that you, Srulek?' Juzek asked. At least he hadn't forgotten my name.

'Juzek', I whispered, 'as an old friend, can you help me get out of here?'

'I'll see after my duty. I'll have a word with the captain', he promised.

That afternoon there was a disturbance in the corridor, with keys rattling and cell doors opening and closing. Then our cell was opened and by the door was a guard I hadn't seen before. Then Juzek appeared. 'Srulek! Come with me!' I jumped off the bunk and followed. 'You're going to see the captain', Juzek explained as we walked down the corridor. 'But don't be frightened because you know the captain. I had a word with him and we think we'll be able to help you.'

The captain sat behind his desk as we entered his office, passing two men in civilian clothes on their way out. 'My God, you're Eddy Woźniakowski!', I exclaimed. He used to be a blacksmith where I took my grandfather's horses to be shoed by his father.

'That's right', he answered.

'Is your father still alive?'

'No, he died in 1944.'

'And your mother?'

'She died in January this year. What about your family?'

'They're all dead', I said, 'Karol and I are the only survivors.' Juzek and the captain hung their heads in sorrow.

'I'm very sorry about your family because I knew them as well as you knew mine', I continued. 'The difference is that your family died a natural death and you can visit their graves whenever you want. I haven't got a grave to visit because where most of my family went there were no graves. All the Germans left behind were human ashes they dumped on wet marshland in Treblinka where nearly one million men, women and children were murdered.' I could see they were upset at my story. 'I am also upset about your families because I know everybody knew each other and got along so well.'

'Srulek', the captain said, 'you're free to go.' He and Juzek wished me luck.

'Before I go', I said, 'Can you tell me why I was arrested?'

'We've been watching the house of the woman you went to visit. There are a few houses in Konin with women like her, who collaborated with the Germans and had lots of German children. They're going to be sent across the border to East Germany and classified as German women. You happened to go into that house and no one knew who you were. You were arrested so we could learn the connection between the two of you.'

'The only connection is that we lived next door before the war. I knew her husband when he went into the army and never returned.' I thanked Eddy and Juzek for their help and walked out of the hands of the Polish secret police.

I went straight to the Red Cross for something to eat. Looking for a place to sit in the crowded dining hall, I heard my brother calling my name. I pushed my way to the window, where I found Karol and Henry Kawałek, a friend of mine from before the war. He and two of his uncles had been taken, with Karol and myself, to Auschwitz at the same time. When I was sent to the coal mines at Jaworzno we were separated. Miraculously, Henry was liberated from Mauthausen and, like Karol and me, had found his way back to Konin. (Henry later changed his name to Kaye and he and his wife Sala, also an Auschwitz survivor, later moved to England, where they now live.)

'We were counting the days you were missing. Today is the eleventh day: where have you been?' They had been very worried about me; after all, we were the three youngest survivors out of nearly 3,000 Jewish people lost from Konin.

'I have bad news for you', Karol said. 'You've had a delivery by a military policeman with call-up papers for you to join the Army Cadets of Political Upbringing.'

'Now I'm in trouble. I must find a way to get away from here', I concluded.

24 · Dr Schonfeld

The three of us left the Red Cross, walking through the main street towards Liberty Square. It was August 1945. A Jewish lady and her daughter who knew us stopped us and said to Karol and me: 'I've just come off a train from Łódź and we've been to the Hotel Grand. There's a man in an English officer's uniform there. He has an interpreter who speaks Polish, Yiddish and English. When he heard I was from Konin he asked if I knew of two brothers, Karol and Srulek Hahn. I told him you were still in Konin. He said if I should see you, I should tell you to get on a train for Łódź and come to the Hotel Grand because he wants to see you.'

The three of us stood wondering why this Englishman would ask about us. I saw my old friend Juzek from the secret police coming towards us. 'You won't remember these two but I'll tell you: this is my brother Karol and this is our friend Henry. The three of us came out of the concentration camps.'

'Karol I remember as a little boy', said Juzek.

'You knew Henry as a little boy, too', I reminded him. 'He lived at the back of you, his father was Kawałek the butcher.'

'Of course I remember now.'

'You should – you lived among all the Jewish people. Juzek, I want to show you something.' I unfolded my call-up documents.

'Holy Jesus!', he exclaimed. 'This document means you'll probably have to go to Moscow for training in a cadet school to serve in the Polish secret service.' The more he told me, the more I wanted to run away from Konin. What he was telling me brought back bad memories. Juzek wished us good luck and walked away.

'You know what?', I said. 'I came to the conclusion that there is nothing left for us in Konin except bad memories. Let's take the train to Łódź.' We left immediately. The journey to Łódź took two hours – the trains never hurried in Poland. When we arrived, it was easy enough to find the Hotel Grand.

There were many people waiting to be called into one of the hotel rooms to be interviewed. We had waited an hour and a half when we heard our names. The man who called us asked in Polish: 'Do you speak Yiddish?'

'A few words', I replied. He told us who Dr Schonfeld was as he opened the hotel room door.

Behind a large writing desk was a very handsome man with a tiny beard. He was wearing an English military uniform with red patches on each sleeve; embroidered in white were the words 'Chief Rabbi'. He wore a skull cap. He looked at us over the top of his glasses while he and his interpreter had a conversation which Karol and I couldn't understand.

The interpreter asked us in Yiddish: 'Do you know anybody in England?'

'Yes', I answered. 'There's my grandmother's brother and my grandfather's brother who went to England before the 1914 war; the family was always talking about them. The one I remember most is my mother's sister. She went to England at the beginning of 1939.'

'Do you remember her name?'

'Yes, her name is Gittla Szwiatowicz.'

'That's who's looking for you, your Aunt Gittla in London.'

'When are we going to London?', I asked.

Three-quarters of an hour later the interpreter explained the situation to us. 'Listen, lads, this is the position', he began. 'We have documents here for two of you to go to London. But according to Dr Schonfeld's documents he can only take one of you this time and it has to be the youngest, Karol. I assure you that as soon as possible I will be back and you will be the first on the list to go to London.'

'We were never separated in the concentration camps', I insisted, 'and we don't want to be separated now. We'll come back as soon as you send for us and we can go to London together.'

When we returned some four months later to the Hotel Grand it was packed with Russian and Polish officers. The interpreter gave us the news: 'All your papers are in order and you can travel to London together. Tomorrow morning you will board a train to Warsaw. You'll be met in Warsaw by two people from the Jewish Committee who will escort you to the place where you'll be staying.'

At the station we met up with the other young people travelling to Warsaw. After a long wait in the December cold the train arrived. As usual it was packed with Russian and Polish soldiers, but we managed to find a space for ourselves. Most of us looked out of the windows, bidding our last farewell to Łódź.

The two men from the Jewish Committee met us at the bomb-scarred station in Warsaw. After half an hour's walk we reached a synagogue. Only two halls in the synagogue had survived the German bombing. Many more young people waited inside, sitting on their bunk beds, three tiers high. In the evening a truck arrived with our evening meal of soup and bread from the Jewish Committee. We enjoyed the food, happy to be leaving behind a country full of bad memories and murdered families.

We received news from Dr Schonfeld that we might have to stay in Warsaw for a few more weeks. He had to wait for a Red Cross ship to reach the port of Gdynia which would take us to England. We weren't unhappy in the synagogue. At least we knew we had a destination. We were in Warsaw right through Christmas and the New Year of 1946.

One day we asked a stranger to direct us to the part of town that was once the Jewish ghetto. It was in ruins. Most of the ground was still soaked with blood, Jewish blood spilt by the SS executioners. Not being sure where exactly we were, I stopped an old man on a bicycle. 'Is this where the Jewish ghetto was?'

'Not only was this the Jewish ghetto', he volunteered, 'but the railway track you are standing on was used by the SS to deport all the Jews from the Warsaw ghetto to the gas chambers. The trains went to Treblinka – a place of no return.'

I was curious how he knew all this. 'I used to be employed by the Polish railway authorities, maintaining the railway tracks', he said.

'I am asking you these things because I am a Jew', I told

him. 'Not only that, but my friends here and I are survivors of Auschwitz concentration camp.'

'Holy Jesus!', he mumbled, clutching his cap in his hands. 'I was working a bit further down the line with a bunch of Polish railway men. We watched the way the SS loaded the men, women and children into the goods trains like animals, with the help of their Alsatian dogs. The shooting into the crowd and the screams were unbearable. We had to move further down the line not to hear the screams from the women and children. I wouldn't like to go through that experience again in my lifetime.'

My friends and I agreed that the old man hadn't seen a lot – we had seen much worse. It unnerved us to be in this place of suffering, listening to the old man's story.

One Thursday morning Mr Weinberg picked out five boys and five girls, including me, Karol and and a girl called Erika. He briefed us on what was about to happen. 'You're going to have an interview with the British ambassador. He will want to know the reason you want to go to England.'

Mr Weinberg spoke to the ambassador alone and then called me, Karol, Erika and another girl into his office.

Mr Weinberg said to me: 'The ambassador wants to know why you're wearing army clothes.'

'Tell the ambassador that the army clothes were given to me to replace my prison camp uniform. I simply needed new clothes and these were what was on offer.'

'Were you in the army?', Mr Weinberg interpreted.

'Tell the ambassador I was in the concentration camps', and I showed him the number tattooed on my arm. The ambassador picked up my arm to have a closer look. He said something to Mr Weinberg, who went to my brother and asked to see his arm. The ambassador looked at the number on Karol's arm and shook his head in disbelief.

The ambassador and Mr Weinberg spoke for a few more minutes. Finally Mr Weinberg said: 'You'll be pleased to know that the ambassador has granted you permission to go to London. I'll be at the synagogue early in the morning and I'll give you instructions on what you have to do.'

We walked through the streets of Warsaw in twos, side-stepping the rubble. Mr Weinberg asked if we wanted to go to the Jewish Committee to have something to eat. The Committee had built a kitchen and dining room there which held about 200 people. It was 29 March 1946.

We walked in and Mr Weinberg called for our attention. 'Tomorrow morning, Friday, you are all going to Gdynia. The girls will fly in a small aeroplane and all the boys will go by train.'

The next day I day-dreamed while we were waiting for the train that would take us away. It seemed I had been waiting a week when suddenly I heard the puffing of the train getting nearer and nearer until it stopped in front of me. Everybody on the platform rushed on to the train and I became separated from the rest of the boys in our group. I got on board anyway but I couldn't find a seat; I had to stand in the corridor.

As I stood there, by the door, I looked out of the window and watched as the train pulled away from the station. Most of the passengers got off the train at the first stop. I now had a cabin to myself and began to drift off to sleep. Suddenly the cabin door slid open and in front of me stood a ticket inspector. 'Inspector, I don't have a ticket.'

'And why not?', he asked.

'Because I haven't got any money.'

'Have you just come out of the army?'

'No, a lot worse than coming out of the army.' I showed him my Auschwitz number.

He scratched the back of the head. 'Have a pleasant journey!', he said and he closed the door behind him. The train stopped a few more times and was almost empty by the time we reached Gdynia.

When I got off the train I didn't know where to go. I could see the sea in the distance and headed in that direction. Whatever ship was at the port, I would try and get on it. I didn't even care if the ship wasn't going to England. I just had to get away from Poland.

Fortunately there was only one ship and it was flying a white flag with a Red Cross on it. Once I saw that, I knew someone from the ship would help me. As I reached the gangway I heard a shout: 'Halt!' Three security soldiers were walking towards me. 'Where do you think you're going?', asked the sergeant.

'I'm going on this ship.'

'Have you any papers?'

'No.'

'You can't go on this ship', he said sternly. 'Why are you dressed in uniform?'

'I was in a concentration camp and when I came out I had nothing to wear so a friend of mine, who came out of the army, gave me this old uniform. I have nothing to do with the army.' Here I was with the secret service again. I was like a magnet to a piece of metal. I couldn't help it, I couldn't get civilian clothes.

I heard a cough behind me. There was a sailor standing on the gangway trying to see what was going on. I waved to him hoping he would help me with the security soldiers. He ran down the gangway: 'What's the problem?'

'I am here because I have permission to leave Poland and go to England', I told him.

'Do you know who's taking you to England?'

'Yes, a man on this ship by the name of Dr Schonfeld.'

'You've come to the right place.'

At that moment I saw Karol rushing down the gangway, shouting 'Where've you been?'

'It's a long story.' The sailor explained that, according to the Swedish Red Cross, the security men could only come as far as the gangway. They watched me board the ship and walked away.

Candlesticks stood on a dining-room table with two *chala* breads covered by a white cloth, embroidered with gold Hebrew letters. Dr Schonfeld lit the candles, saying the Sabbath prayer.

When the prayer ended, the Red Cross nurses rushed in with cutlery and dinner plates. Waiters carried silver bowls of kosher chicken soup, roast chicken and roast potatoes. We hadn't seen such food in the last six years: the kitchen was supervised by a very religious Jewish woman.

But I could only think of what we had left behind. Not Poland, but my beloved murdered family. I didn't expect anyone to understand that feeling of pain. We were tired after such a long day, so we went to our cabins with the candles still burning on the dining-room table.

I was awakened by the ship's engines and the waves beating against the side of the ship. I thought I was dreaming. I got dressed and made my way to the top deck. I watched the ship sail into the darkness. Everything was going through my mind at once. From the day the Germans occupied my home town of Konin and how they had murdered my entire family in cold blood. The further the ship sailed, the more I wept silently.

When I opened the cabin door my brother switched on the light: 'Are we sailing?'

'Yes.' He started sobbing. I started crying too but I tried to control myself, so as not to encourage Karol. 'Why don't you stop crying?'

'I can't stop! Look what we're leaving behind – our whole family. I can't stop thinking about them.' Both of us wept. Between sobs I heard him say: 'I wish I had gone with Mother and Father and our brother and sister on the train to the Treblinka gas chambers.'

'Stop crying and don't be silly.' All night we sat up talking. It wasn't until we saw the sun rising through the porthole that we finally fell asleep on our bunks.

The only thing I wasn't happy about were the clothes I was wearing. One of my friends said he had a pair of trousers that would fit me and another said I could have one of his jackets. I thanked the two of them for helping me get rid of the Polish military clothes. I felt like a free man again.

25 · A New Life in London

I watched as we sailed towards a great bridge the like of which I'd never seen before: it seemed that there were castles at the very centre of it. Then the bridge started to move, one piece breaking away from the other. I noticed what looked like a castle across the river. We all guessed it must be London.

It was about two hours before we left the ship. The interpreter said: 'Those who haven't got anyone to meet them, please get on the bus.' There were a lot of us who got on the bus, but most went away with their relatives in private cars. The streets were full of traffic – trams, taxis and over-sized red buses – and people. Eventually we arrived at a beautiful tree-lined street just like in Poland and stopped outside a big mansion.

Dr Schonfeld said: 'You've reached your destination here in London. You are welcome in this hostel. It's run by myself and some colleagues. Everything will be alright. We have prepared food for you, but before we eat, please sit down while I say a few words of prayer.'

After a couple of weeks I realized the hostel was an institution of sorts. They wanted to bring us up as religious Jews. I was very depressed. I thought my aunt had abandoned us.

As we were walking out of the hostel gate one day we saw a woman walking towards us. Something about her shook me. I was seeing my mother in the face of this stranger and I realized it was my aunt. She went to the front desk at the hostel and talked to the man there. 'This is my aunt', I interrupted them.

'How do you know I'm your aunt?'

'Because you look so much like my mother', I insisted.

'Perhaps I do, perhaps I don't.'

I asked her: 'Why are you denying that you are our aunt and our mother's sister? Your name is Gittla.'

'How do you know you are my nephews?', she said coldly. 'What is your father's name?' I told her. 'And what is your mother's name?' I told her that too. 'What about your father and mother? Your father is my grandfather, you missed them out', I snapped. 'Don't ask me any more questions, let me tell you some names and we'll see if you still remember them. You have been away from home a long time, since before the war even began. Tell me, who is Ludwik Szwiatowicz and Rivka Szwiatowicz? And what about your younger sister Golda?'

Tears welled in her eyes, but I continued: 'I'll give you better clues. You lived in Danzig in 1939 when Germany started the trouble about Danzig belonging to Germany. You sent all your furniture home to Konin by train. Me, my father, my grandfather and your brothers David and Revuz all went to the station with a horse and cart to collect the furniture and take it to my grandfather's house. I will even tell you the colour of the furniture. The beds, wardrobes and dressing tables had carved legs and were painted black; everything else was painted white.'

She burst into tears. I put my hand on her shoulder. 'I'm glad you understand what I'm saying. When I look at you, I see my mother over and over again. Now you know who we are, will you take us with you?'

'Yes', she said softly. 'I'll have a word with the man.' She went to the office and after about 20 minutes she returned and said we could go with her.

She took us by bus to Aldgate East, an area in east London. We walked to Wentworth Street, where she lived on the second floor in a block of flats.

We sat at the dining-room table as she asked about our family. She cried as I spoke and Karol and I felt we too were about to cry, but we couldn't. Something inside wouldn't let us. Even though my voice was wavering I let her carry on asking questions and I had to tell her what I knew, where everybody was. Can you imagine telling her she had no family? And can you imagine she could accept the explanation? She kept saying: 'I don't believe it. I don't believe it.'

'I'm afraid it's the truth. I was there and we can't change anything. We have to get on with our lives. You don't believe it, but we do because we witnessed it with our own eyes. You can't believe it because you lived and worked with the Germans in Danzig. But when Hitler took over as chancellor it was a different Germany. Then your trouble started anyway and you had to get rid of all your things and send them to my grandfather. You had to run away to England. You must try to understand that the Germans turned into different people from the ones you knew. From 1939 to 1945, people outside knew what was happening, but no one wanted to help us. No one did help us until Hitler invaded Poland.'

I stopped because I was so upset. Aunt Gittla was crying into her handkerchief.

After a few weeks at our new jobs in a ladies' overcoat factory (before that, we'd worked at a pram factory) we told Aunt Gittla that we wanted to live on our own. She was very cross. Her idea was that we should stay with her and save enough money to buy a house and she would look after us for ever.

Eventually Karol and I found separate lodgings close to one another. I changed my name from Srulek to Isaac – Issy for short.

One day, completely out of the blue, Aunt Gittla said we had murdered our entire family. I felt like I had been stabbed through the heart with a dagger. When I told Karol what she had said he exclaimed with tears pouring down his face: 'I'm not going to see her any more. How could she say we killed our family?' My brother couldn't forgive her for this and never went to see her again. I myself couldn't resist visiting her because she reminded me so much of my mother. (Gittla Szwiatowicz, born in Konin in 1900, passed away in London at the age of 85.)

I found a place, Sid's Café, where I went for my evening meals. Sid had made his home in London after being liberated from Mauthausen. He remained a good friend of mine. (When he passed away, his sister, also a survivor, had his body flown to America to be with the rest of his family.)

One day when I showed up at Sid's, I was surprised to see Jakob, the *Kapo* from Leitmeritz. He was performing at the Royal Albert Hall as strongman 'Samson'. I was pleased Jakob had survived the camps. He had moved to Israel after the war where he had married and had two children. (Jakob lived out the rest of his life in America.)

During this time I tried to recapture some of my lost teenage years. Some of the boys from Poland and my new English friends began visiting dance halls. For half-a-crown, you could hear the best swing bands in London. I loved the music and my new life. I even did some acting and singing in the Yiddish Theatre.

I would meet friends opposite the Grand Palais dance hall to catch the Number 25 bus to the West End. One evening I saw a beautiful girl walk past. I asked her if she wanted to go out with me and I think she was a little surprised by my forwardness. She told me she was going dancing and if I wanted to see her I would have to wait until she came home.

I waited. A few months later, on 1 May 1947, Lena and I were married. One year later we had our first child, Stanley, named after my father. The next year our daughter Helen, who was named after my mother, was born. Five years later we had our son David, named after my mother's brother who was the Konin taxi driver. Our family was complete.

During the early years of our married life I found a job with a wholesale butcher, Sidney Ziff & Co., delivering meat. By the end of my career with the company I had worked my way up to abattoir manager.

Life was good. Karol married a pretty Welsh girl named Margaret and they had two daughters of their own, Louise and Melissa. I felt rewarded when my grandchildren were born, pleased I had grandsons to carry on the name and traditions of my murdered family.

I carried on, pretending I was a happy man. But it is not easy to forget the past. Whenever I was asked about the war I put on a brave face. I didn't expect anyone to understand unless they had been in the same situation. Karol and I got on with our lives and the years went by.

Epilogue

In May 1987, I received an unexpected telephone call. The caller, Theo Richmond, told me he was writing a book about Konin and would like to meet me. When we met, Theo explained that many members of his family had originated in Konin and had died in the death camps; as a small boy living in London, he had heard a great deal about the place. He had been travelling around the world gathering information for his book and was now about to make a journey to Konin itself. I was no less keen than he was to visit the place where I was born and we agreed to make the trip to Konin together.

We left for Poland that summer for an 11-day stay. On the plane for Warsaw, as we flew lower and lower, a cold sensation came over me. Theo understood the pain I felt – he too had lost so many members of his family in the Holocaust.

Our first destination was the *Um Schlagplatz*. Our taxi stopped in front of a marble wall inscribed in golden letters. The marble monument bore the names of families who had been deported from the ghetto to Treblinka. The site was now watched over by an old woman with a collection box.

Our taxi driver told us about an underground shelter which had been preserved as a memorial. He stopped in front of a large green mound planted with trees and there were wooden benches where people were sunning themselves. We walked across the green to the former shelter. On its side was a bronze plaque which read: 'In this place, the hero Mordechai Anielewicz, the leader of the Jewish Resistance, died fighting against German SS troops.'

Our driver told us the story of Mordechai Anielewicz: 'He was born in Warsaw and died a young man of 24. When the Germans were closing in on this underground shelter he sent his officers out to save themselves, telling them to escape through the underground sewer while he held off the SS troops with a machine gun. He ran out of ammunition and at the last moment shot himself rather than be captured or shot by the SS.'

The next morning, Theo and I took the train to Konin. As the train slowed on its approach to the town, the conductor shouted out: 'Konin Station! Konin Station!' We stepped on to the platform. I saw nothing that was familiar to me.

We drove through the main street of Kleczew, several miles to the north-west of Konin, and stopped a man to ask for directions. We wanted to meet a woman living in the town. 'You mean Auntie?', the man enquired.

'Who's Auntie?', I asked.

'The only Jewish woman still alive of all the people in the town. Go to the corner of that street – it's the first door.'

At first Auntie wouldn't open the door: I saw her peep through the window. Finally she opened up. 'Do you remember Karol and David Szwiatowicz?', I asked right away, 'they were my uncles. Why were you afraid to open the door?', I continued.

It seems that a group of Polish boys had recently smeared cow dung and written anti-Jewish slogans on her windows. A few weeks before we arrived the police had arrested the boys, who had been given prison sentences. Our driver, Felix, couldn't believe that boys like that still existed so many years after the war; he was very upset.

'What is your first name?', I asked Auntie.

'My name is Hannah.'

'Tell me, is the synagogue still here or has it been demolished?'

Hannah took us into the street and showed us where the synagogue had stood. 'If you look at that building where the people are now living, that's where the Germans demolished the synagogue, but left the public baths. The Germans brought the Jewish people – truck after truck of men, women and children – from all the districts around Kleczew and forced them into the baths. There were two trucks with long pipes connected from the baths to the exhausts of the trucks. When the baths were full of people the SS men shut the doors and one of them signalled to the drivers of the trucks and they started their engines. As the exhaust fumes filled the baths you could hear the people screaming for help, especially the children. After a while the screaming stopped.'

'What happened to all the bodies?'

'They had hostages in the old Polish police station who were made to load up the bodies and they took them to Kazimierz forest.'

'When did you find out exactly what happened in Kleczew?', I asked.

'I was hiding with a Polish family. I married one of their sons but he passed away in 1960. You remember Stefan Rogowski? He lived at the back of the synagogue and saw everything. He couldn't believe what he saw. There were a few other people too who knew about it.'

Auntie held my arm as we walked back to her house. 'When I first married I had to change my religion and become a Christian.'

'Did changing your religion help you?', I asked curiously.

'Yes. I used to go to church every Sunday and all the people in the town showed me a great deal of respect. I had peace and quiet until those boys started on me.'

About a mile out of town, in Wilków, was Konin Catholic cemetery. An old woman was selling flowers outside the gate. I asked her where we would find the solitary Jewish grave. She gave me directions to a large mass grave.

The Jewish cemetery was demolished by the Germans, with the help of prisoners from the Konin labour camp at Czarkow. It was left to the Polish people to bury the Jewish victims, so they buried them in their own cemetery. A large granite memorial stone with the Star of David carved on it marked the grave. It was tended personally by the Polish superintendent of the cemetery.

As I looked around I found many graves of people I had known before the war; many of them had their photographs in porcelain on the headstones. I felt sorry for them because most of them had died as young people during the war.

We made our way to 3 May Street. There I saw a small café on the site of the posh restaurant that had belonged to Aleksander Kurowski. Kurowski had been executed together with the Jewish religious man, Mordechai Slodki, in front of the old gymnasium shortly after the Germans' arrival in Konin.

The next morning I wanted to find the wooden plaque some of us had erected in Kazimierz forest after the war in memory of those murdered there. We searched for the memorial without success. Then I noticed a man on a bicycle watching us. He offered us his help.

'Do you know where there are any graves?', I asked him.

'Yes, there are five graves.'

'Do you know much about them? You look too young to remember what happened here.'

'I know enough from my grandparents and my parents. I was born after the war, but sometimes the whole of our family would sit around the table and talk about how the Germans murdered the Jewish men, women and children in this forest. My grandparents used to tell me about the shooting. You could hear the echo of the screams for miles, especially the screams of the children. They said it was so unbearable that they had to get on their horse and cart with the whole family and travel miles to avoid the screaming echoes in the forest. If you look and listen you won't see or hear any birds in this forest. They migrated at the time of the shooting and built their nests in other forests. We also had a lot of deer in this forest; they never returned either. So you see, this forest is as dead as the people in those graves.

'After the war, people came from all over to pick blackberries and mushrooms. One day my grandfather heard shouts of excitement echo through the forest from boys and girls picking mushrooms. When he went to see what all the shouting was about, the children showed him a handful of gold wedding rings. One of the girls said that when they were looking in the bushes, she came across a cluster of mushrooms growing together. On top of the mushrooms lay the gold rings. The children didn't know where they had come from, but my grandfather did. He said they had come from the screaming women the Germans had murdered. My grandfather couldn't understand how the gold rings were found lying on top of the mushrooms.'

As the rings had laid on the forest floor the mushrooms had

grown and pushed them up as if presenting them to the sky. I can think of only two explanations', I said. 'The first is that the women saw what was happening and realized that they were about to die. The executioners were taking all the jewellery from the women and, instead of giving the SS the satisfaction of having their wedding rings, they took them off their fingers and hid them in the bushes. The second explanation could be that in the Jewish religion, you come into this world with nothing and you should go out with nothing.'

Theo had the name and address of a vet who had witnessed the executions in Kazimierz forest. When we met the vet noticed my Auschwitz tattoo and called to his wife and daughter to show them my arm. I asked the vet about his experience in the Kazimierz forest.

In October 1945, the vet said, the chairman of the Konin court had arranged a court hearing near the mass graves in the forest. They had also called as a witness a man named Aleksander Ciborski, who knew the forest very well. The condition of the mass graves was recorded and details kept in the court in Konin. The vet was called to give evidence, as an eyewitness, in connection with the executions in the forest. The vet told us what he had seen:

'I had to tell the court exactly what happened. It was 1941 and it was a very cold night. A Gestapo man came to the prison where I had been held as a hostage for several weeks, and told me to prepare myself for a journey. They chained my hands and took me and other hostages, put us on a truck and drove to the railway station.

'I was able to see which road we took because the tarpaulin on the back of the truck was rolled up. We were travelling on the road to Golin; from there the truck took the road towards Kazimierz forest, which I recognized. As we rode along the forest path we said to ourselves: this is where we're going to die, this is going to be our cemetery.

'They unchained us and told us to stand with our backs to the forest path. Then they marched 30 or so of us prisoners deep into the forest. We came upon two huge dug-out pits with groups of people standing around – men and women with children in their arms. The pits had quicklime at the bottom.

170

'The Gestapo who took us there said we would see how they dealt with the Jews and if we didn't like it and tried to escape, we'd be shot. Then they ordered the people to strip. We were ordered to collect all their jewellery. When they saw what was happening, the people started throwing their rings and other objects of value as far as they could into the forest.

'By the time we had collected the jewellery the people were all standing naked. The Gestapo told us to hand over the rings and watches and the officers stuffed them into their uniform pockets. Then they ordered the women holding babies to jump into the pits partially filled with quicklime. At the same time, there were two German water tankers, one on each side of the pit, with thick hoses, pumping water into the pit. I cannot describe the screams of the women and children as they jumped into the pit; they were being boiled alive. The cries were so terrible that the SS were shooting them in the pit.

'We were ordered to sort out the clothing. We could hear the cries so loud, it was terrible to hear. We tore pieces of cloth and stuffed them in our ears to shut out the screams of the people being boiled alive. When they had executed all the people they gathered us all together, gave us shovels and made us shovel the earth into the graves to cover up the dead bodies.

'Then they put us on the trucks again and took us back to the prison. I was in there for another five weeks. At night I could still hear the screams of those poor people in the pit. After five more weeks we were taken in a cattle train to Mauthausen concentration camp. I was there until I was liberated in 1945. Unfortunately most of my friends, with whom I was in the Konin prison, did not survive the camp.'

When we left the vet we made our way to the Konin park, at the end of which was a small gate. We walked through it and across the road. There was a small wood there which had once been the site of the Jewish cemetery. The Polish communist government had shown its utter disregard for the Jewish graves by planting pine trees on top of them. When you looked closely at the ground you could see red brick protruding out. This is what remained of the foundation of a headstone.

171

Outside the cemetery there was a gigantic monument commemorating the Polish people who had been executed on this spot. We walked back through the park towards Market Square. On our way there we went down a street in which we saw a large, picturesque cottage standing in the middle of a garden. I remembered the couple who had lived here with their son and daughter. During the war the son had volunteered for the Ukrainian army and the parents had been transported to Ostrowiec. There the Gestapo had given them a large shop in which they had sold shoe leather. You could only get this leather with a permit from the German mayor of the town. They had lived in a bungalow in front of my aunt and uncle's house. They were the people who had informed on us to the German police.

'Is this Czarkow?', Theo asked as we walked back to the hotel. 'I was told that there is a Jewish cemetery here that is 300 or 400 years old.' We walked on a bit further then stopped.

We had reached the Jewish cemetery Theo spoke of. The Jewish concentration camp had been in the field nearby. In 1937 I had heard people talking about the cemetery. That part of the field was sold to a private owner. It had been discovered that next to the cemetery, deep down under the ground, were gravel pits, and they wanted to dig for the gravel. The town's Jewish Committee was consulted about the site of the cemetery, and the rabbi and the Committee decided that the remains from the cemetery had to be dug up and transported to the main Jewish cemetery in Konin.

One day I was sitting in my grandfather's house when there was a knock on the door. There were two men there. They asked my grandfather if they could use his horses to pull the hearse that would transport the bodies from the cemetery. My grandfather agreed and they asked how much they owed him, but he wouldn't take any money. He said he would do it in honour of the dead.

My grandfather asked how they intended to transport the bodies to the main cemetery. The men explained that the rabbi had decided that the remains in each grave would have to be put into a pure white linen bag under religious supervision.

I remember taking the two horses to the hearse. There was

a man there who was capable of handling the horses and the hearse. The man knew who I was so he let me help him hitch up the horses. When I looked in the back of the hearse, it was already loaded with bundles of white linen bags. I went up on the front of the hearse and sat next to the driver as we made our way there.

When we got there there were plenty of people who had volunteered to load the bags of remains on to the hearse. It took three or four days until everything was cleared, including the memorial headstones. When I went back a couple of weeks later, work had already begun on the gravel pits.

Theo had the address of a museum just outside Konin that he wanted to visit. 'I know it, but not as a museum', I told him. 'It was a sugar refinery belonging to a wealthy Polish landowner. He had hundreds of acres on which he grew sugar beet.'

The next day we drove to the country mansion in Goslawice only five or six miles from Konin. I couldn't believe I was in the mansion that had once belonged to the Polish nobleman Stanisław Hwilecki.

We wandered among the exhibits of Jewish history and prehistoric animals found in the area. I told a museum official that I remembered the nobleman who had lived in the mansion. He used to come to Konin in a small, custom-built American car; he wore rimless glasses and held a sword in his hand. The man didn't remember the nobleman but had heard similar stories from his father and grandfather. I asked him what had become of the man.

'It's a very tragic story', he began. 'One day the Gestapo came and dragged the nobleman from his home. The people working in the mansion gardens saw him being beaten right in front of their eyes, but they couldn't help him. The next day some of the local villagers found out that the Gestapo were torturing the Polish intelligentsia.

'The Gestapo put some of the prisoners in an army truck and drove them through the park to a small gate. As the prisoners got off the truck they were hit over the head. The prisoners ran through the small gate, shielding themselves with their hands, straight to the Jewish cemetery and straight into the hands of the waiting Gestapo execution squads. They shot them one by one. That brought to an end the life of the nobleman and his family. They brought in Jewish prisoners to prepare the burial, under the supervision of the Gestapo.' He added that the entire episode had been witnessed by a boy, hiding in the bushes, who had lived nearby.

So the big memorial in front of the Jewish cemetery was for these Polish people who had been executed, among them the nobleman and his family.

Theo completed his book some six years after our trip to Konin. I was proud when the final result was so well received worldwide. It was important for *Konin: A Quest* (Vintage 1996) to be written. It is a documentation of how Konin's 3,000 Jews vanished from the face of the earth at the hands of the Germans. A portrait of everyday town life over the centuries.

As for myself, I did not survive by sheer luck. At times, I was stupid enough to believe that my brother and I might be the only two people to survive. But we wanted to live, not only for ourselves – we had already lost all that was dear to us – but to tell the world what Hitler's SS was capable of. When I was fighting for my own survival I had to block out the memory of my family. Now they are with me constantly. I am left with a life sentence of memories.

I wouldn't let anything stand in my way. You had to be very alert and devious, especially when there was a selection of prisoners for deportation. You had to make the right decision. Which line should you follow? If you joined the wrong line, there was only one way for you to go – the road of no return.

What differentiates me from the six million Jews who were killed? Thousands of Jews died every day for five years in the gas chambers and in mass shootings, but survivors like me have been slowly dying inside for over 50 years as a result of the suffering the Nazis inflicted on us. They murdered not only Jews but Polish Christians too. Thousands of Polish hostages were executed daily among the ruins in Warsaw. In virtually every street in Warsaw brass plaques mounted on walls provide details of the number of people who were exterminated on that spot.

There are not enough words and there is certainly not enough money in this world to put these atrocities right. They must never be forgotten. They must serve as a warning to mankind.